Atlanta History
For Cocktail Parties II,
Another Round

James M. Ottley

Copyright© 2013 James M. Ottley

ISBN: 978-1-300-70249-8

Foreword:

In my mid-twenties, I read from cover-to-cover Franklin Garrett's comprehensive history of Atlanta, entitled: *Atlanta and Environs: A Chronicle of Its People and Events*. I found it fascinating, but realized many readers would not have the time or, perhaps interest, to read the entire text since it is over 3,000 pages long, is comprised of three volumes and contains almost every detail of Atlanta's history. It is truly a work of art and it unequivocally established Franklin Garrett as Atlanta's official historian.

I thought it a worthy endeavor to attempt a synopsis of Garrett's work to make the highlights available to readers with a more casual interest in Atlanta history. In the first volume of *Atlanta History for Cocktail Parties*, I tackled the first volume of Garrett's work. In that endeavor, I sought to extract what I felt to be the most interesting events and facts with the hope that this might in turn inspire some readers to learn more about Atlanta history. In this book, I have attempted to accomplish the same task working primarily from Garrett's second volume of *Atlanta and Environs*. I am eternally grateful to the University of Georgia Press for granting me permission to reprint portions of the Garrett text and to Frederick Allen and Tommy H. Jones for allowing me to reprint quotes from their works as well.

The stated purpose of this book is to be a moderately interesting account of some of the more unique, odd and even trivial goings-on in Atlanta's history related primarily from Garrett's account. The content comprises a series of stories that I found interesting enough to risk recounting at cocktail parties. As such, it is not intended to be a comprehensive or congruent account of Atlanta's history.

I sincerely hope that you enjoy this collection of factoids, trivia and anecdotes and that you are drawn to further investigate Atlanta's rich history.

TABLE OF CONTENTS

    Page No.

"Oh Lawd, Just Make Sure I am Presentable When Patterson's Comes to Get Me"	9
The Spelman-Rockefeller Connection	10
For the Record: Grant Park	11
Lawyer Glut in Atlanta Leads Woodrow Wilson to Politics	14
Five Things You Probably Did Not Know About The *Atlanta Journal* (Now The *Atlanta Journal & Constitution*)	15
How a Crowded Pool Room Led to the Creation of the Capital City Club	15
Tomb with a View	16
The Five Points Artesian Well	17
At Least the Gold on the Gold Dome is From Georgia	17
Haverty's Makes Its Home	18
Atlanta's Cyclorama Was Originally Displayed in the Motor City	19
"They're Healing Me With Science"	21
Fort McPherson Originally to be Named Fort Hancock	22
A Coke is Born	22
Once in a While You Get Shown the Light in the Strangest of Places if You Look at it Right	26
Coca-Cola, B.C.	27

Fish Don't Fry in the Kitchen, Beans Don't Burn on the Grill	28
Is There Cocaine in it?	30
Coca-Cola Bottling: Candler Did Indeed Give Away the Rights	34
The Coca-Cola Bottle: Cacao is It!	35
Keeping Track: The History of Piedmont Park	37
Tech Talk: The Origins of Georgia Tech	40
The First Atlanta Zoo Was a Real Circus	42
What Fertilizer, Florida and Yellow Fever Have to do with Agnes Scott College	43
Contrary to What We Told the IOC, Atlanta Does Need One of These: Atlanta's First Sewer System	44
College Park: A Lot for a Name	45
Passing Grady	46
The Craigie House	47
Peachtree by Another Name Would Have Been Grand	51
The 1895 Cotton States and International Exposition	51
When Football Was Banned in Atlanta	52
Woodruff at Woodward	53
What Steel Hoops For Cotton Bales Has To Do With Atlantic Station	53
Bishop Brown's College	53
Atlanta Gets the Bird, and other Cliff Clavin-worthy Trivia	54

Hotel Fires Prior to and Including the Winecoff	55
Famous Landmarks	56
You Can Bank on it	57
Neighborhood Naissance	58
Early Churches	59
Multiple Mansions	60
The House that Jack Built	61
Historic Hotels: More Than You Can Bare	62
Development of Avondale Estates Funded by Drug Money	62
If It Could Grow as Hard as it Could Blow	63
Can You Envision It?	64
Clearly This Must Have Gone Off Without a Hitch	64
The History of Atlanta History	64
Before the iPhone	66
Landing an Airport	66
Because Parents Didn't Have Xanax Back Then	67
Too Big to Flail	68
How Roswell Got Stuck With Fulton County Taxes	68
Lenox Square (Formerly Joyeuse Estate) Scene of First Executive Kidnapping	68

The Back Story on Gone With The Wind	70
Famous Roads	71
Gone With The Wind Factoids	72
In Search of Scarlett	73
Famous Guests of Atlanta's Alcatraz	74
Hermi's Bridge	74
The Low-Down on the High	76
Pre-Piedmont and Early Emory	76
The Candler Building, Worth a Closer Look	77
Piedmont Driving Club Almost *Ansley Park* Driving Club	79
The Grove Park Inn - William Randolph Hearst - Atlanta Connection	79
Why We Won't See a Streetcar in the Median of Ponce de Leon Avenue	80
When Did Peachtree Get So Wide?	80
Two Places in the Atlanta Area Not Named After a Peach Tree	80
You Can Pin This One on Flinn	81
Peachtree Heights Park Formerly Part of Wesley Gray Collier Estate	81
"Ain't Paying No 50 Cents for No Golf" and Other Atlanta Golf Course Trivia	82
The Wren's Nest	82

Monumental Intersection	83
The Oglethorpe-Hearst Connection	84
Tales of the Crypt	84
The Leo Frank Case	84
Fed Up Down South	90
The Cotton Standard	90
Emory University: Mother of Georgia Tech	91
The Role of Candler in Emory's Becoming a University	92
A Dark Period in Atlanta History	93
Egleston Does Right By the Kids	94
Made in Atlanta, the Hanson Motor Car	95
From the Don't Try This at Home Files	96
The Decider: The Man Who Laid Out Peachtree Road	96
George Washington Collier and Ansley Park	97
That Old House	99
Atlanta Hosts Georgia's Three Governors Controversy	101
Appendix I: First-Person Account of the Kidnapping	

"Oh Lawd, Just Make Sure I Am Presentable When Patterson's Comes to Get Me."

For many prominent Atlantans, the *sweet chariot coming for to carry one home* was a Patterson's hearse which stopped off at Spring Hill for a brief stint along the way. The founder of Patterson & Sons Funeral Home, Hyatt M. Patterson, arrived in Atlanta in 1881 from Cleveland County, Ohio.[1] He went to work for undertaker George R. Boaz who also owned a livery stable.[2] Patterson started Patterson's in 1883, and established his professional mark when he handled the funeral of Alexander N. Stephens.[3] Hyatt Patterson died in October, 1923, at which that time his son, Frederick W. Patterson, who had been working with him for some time, took over the business.[4] It was Frederick Patterson who built Spring Hill funeral home at Spring and Tenth Streets in 1928, where it continues to operate to this day.[5]

Opened in 1928 by Frederick Patterson, Spring Hill Funeral Home has handled the funerals of many prominent Atlantans. Frederick Patterson took over the family business from his father, Hyatt M. Patterson, who arrived in Atlanta in 1881.

The Spelman-Rockefeller Connection:

The story of Spelman College began when New Englanders Sophia B. Packard and Harriet Giles decided to organize a seminary for African-American women in 1880.[6]

Packard and Giles believed burgeoning Atlanta would be a good location for their school.[7] When they arrived in Atlanta, Dr. Joseph T. Robert, president of the Atlanta Baptist Seminary (later Morehouse College), suggested they meet with Rev. Frank Quarles, pastor of Friendship Baptist Church, to discuss their idea.[8] According to legend, when Packard and Giles went to the church to find Rev. Quarles, he was in the sanctuary praying for the Lord to send help to Atlanta's African-American women and children.[9] Their knock interrupted his prayer. The Reverend interpreted their arrival as a direct answer to this prayer.[10] The school opened April 11, 1881, in the Friendship Baptist Church basement on the corner of Mitchell and Haynes streets with 11 pupils.[11]

John D. Rockefeller, Sr. became involved with the school in 1882, when Packard and Giles made a pitch for funds in his church in Cleveland, Ohio.[12] At approximately the same time, the school obtained an option to purchase property in West End. By 1884, though, they still had not raised the necessary funds to purchase the property. Fortunately, that same year, the Rockefeller family visited the school and was so impressed that they donated funds for the property and additional facilities.[13] This was particularly fortunate because the school had already moved to the new West End location.[14] The name of the school was changed at that time to Spelman Seminary in honor of Lucy Henry Spelman, the mother of Mrs. Rockefeller.[15]

Rockefeller Hall was erected in 1886 and Packard Hall in 1888.[16] The name was later changed to Spelman College in 1924, since most of the high school level curriculum had been dropped in favor of college work.[17]

For the Record: Grant Park:

Grant Park was *not* named after Civil War General (and later President) Ulysses S. Grant. After the City of Atlanta lost its original park around 1870 due to a deed restriction, it was a city without a park. Colonel Lemuel Pratt Grant owned a large estate which encompassed the area of east Atlanta where Grant Park is located. Grant stepped up and donated 100 acres of his estate to the city on May 17, 1883, with a right of reversion should the land ever be used for other purposes.[18] Grant also sold the City of Atlanta the property on which Grady Hospital is located at a price below market value and contributed thousands of dollars to the hospital.[19]

Grant came to Atlanta in 1840 as a railroad engineer. After serving as a chief engineer in the Confederate army, he later became president of the Atlanta and West Point Railway and the Western Railroad of Alabama.[20]

As chief engineer in the Confederate Army, Grant "designed the defensive fortifications for the city [of Atlanta], a portion of which survive nearby in Grant Park."[21]

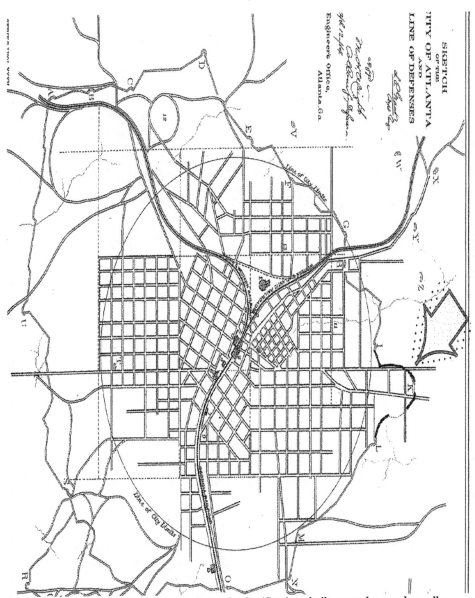

The first Atlanta "beltline," this map shows the fortifications built around a much smaller City of Atlanta. The fortifications were designed and built by L. P. Grant. A portion of the fortifications still survive near Grant Park. (Image courtesy of the Atlanta Preservation Center).

Legend has it that Grant's mansion, located at 727 St. Paul Avenue near Grant Park, was spared in 1864, "because Federal soldiers found a Masonic apron in a trunk in the attic, and Gen. William T. Sherman forbade the burning of property connected with the Masons."[22] The first floor of the house remains today and has been restored by the Atlanta Preservation Center, whose headquarters is now located there. One more interesting fact: the Grant Mansion was the 1902 birthplace of legendary golfer Bobby Jones whose family was staying with the Grants as long-term house guests.[23] Yet another connection, Atlanta tennis legend Bryan M. "Bitsy" Grant, Jr. was the great-grandson of Lemuel Pratt Grant. Grant won the U.S. Clay Court Championship in 1930, 1934, and 1935, and was known as the "Mighty Atom."[24]

The first floor of the L.P. Grant mansion located in the Grant Park neighborhood was, after decades of neglect, spared from destruction by the Atlanta Preservation Center and now serves as its headquarters.

The L.P. Grant Mansion, located in the Grant Park neighborhood was spared in 1864 because Union troops found a Masonic apron in the attic. Only the first floor remains (see photo on page 13).

Lawyer Glut in Atlanta Leads Woodrow Wilson to Politics:

In 1882, after recuperating from an illness in Wilmington, N.C., Woodrow Wilson, then 25, moved to Atlanta to start a law practice.[25] Wilson had attended Davidson College and Princeton University and had obtained a law degree from the University of Virginia.[26] In Atlanta, he joined forces with Edward Ireland Renick, a former classmate at the University of Virginia who had already hung out a shingle. Their partnership, Renick & Wilson, was located in the old Ivan Allen Marshall Building at the corner of Marietta and Forsyth streets.[27] Unfortunately, there were already 143 lawyers practicing in Atlanta at the time, "providing every two hundred and seventy of the population…with a legal advocate."[28] As a result, the partnership was short lived and Wilson gave up the practice of law to enroll in Johns Hopkins University in Baltimore to pursue a doctorate in political science. During his time in Atlanta, though, he met Ellen Axson of Rome, Georgia, whom he married in 1885.[29]

Five Things You Probably Did Not Know About The *Atlanta Journal* (Now The *Atlanta Journal & Constitution*):

The *Atlanta Journal* was an innovator in several ways. The newspaper was founded by Edward F. Hoge, a "native East Tennessean, Confederate Soldier, ex-member of the Legislature from Fulton County and attorney at law."[30] The first edition was printed on February 24, 1883, at 14 West Alabama Street.[31] It became the first newspaper in the South to have a page devoted solely to women's interests, a sports section (as of 1901) and a Sunday magazine (as of 1912).[32] In 1922, it became the first paper in the South, and the second in the nation, to open its own radio station, WSB which stands for "Welcome South Brother."[33] The familiar three-note chime used by NBC promotions was originally used by WSB. James M. Cox, "former governor of Ohio, Democratic candidate for president in 1920, and owner of newspapers in Dayton and Springfield, Ohio and Miami, Florida" purchased the Journal in 1939 for $3,156,350.00, thus establishing the longstanding Cox communications connection to this city.[34]

How a Crowded Pool Room Led to the Creation of the Capital City Club:

In the 1880's, the lobby and billiard rooms of the Kimball House were the preferred meeting places of Atlanta's young men.[35] The Kimball House was a six-story hotel located on Pryor Street, between Decatur and Wall streets. It was in many ways "the public face of Reconstruction-area Atlanta."[36] It was the first building in Atlanta to have elevators and central heating.[37] One evening it was so crowded that four young men, Arch Orme, Joe Orme, Lewis Redwine and Barton M. Blount, could barely find a place to stand.[38] The four went upstairs to Joe and Arch Orme's room and discussed the possibility of starting their own social club.[39] The idea gained traction and the Capital City Club was chartered in April 17, 1883; it was the city's first social club.[40] Their timing was pretty good. The Kimball House was destroyed by fire in the early morning hours of August 12, 1883, the result of a "careless cigar-smoking lemon dealer."[41] The second Kimball House was built on the same site and re-opened New Years Day, 1885.[42] It lasted until 1959, when it was torn down and replaced with a parking deck. During its first five years, the Capital City Club leased a residence located at 43 Walton Street on the southeast corner of its intersection with Fairlie Street.[43] It later relocated to another residence at 114 Peachtree Street at the corner of Peachtree and Ellis Streets.[44] Some of the more notable guests entertained at the club were Jefferson Davis, President Grover Cleveland, President William McKinley and President Howard Taft.[45]

On December 16, 1911, the club moved to its present location at Peachtree and Harris streets. In 1912, the club leased with an option to buy the land where the club's intown golf course, known as Brookhaven, is located.[46] The club exercised its option and purchased the property between 1913 and 1914.[47] The original golf course at Brookhaven was only nine holes, but was increased later to 18.[48]

Tomb With A View:

Oakland Cemetery was known until 1876 as the "City Cemetery." By 1884, it was close to full capacity and local Atlantans were dying to get a plot there.[49] As a result, a group of leading citizens chartered the West View Cemetery Company, and purchased the nucleus of the present Westview cemetery, which comprised 577 acres, for $25,000.[50] Garrett writes that "[o]nly twenty years before, on June 28, 1864, part of the ground had run red with the blood of Confederate and Union soldiers during the hotly contested battle of Ezra Church."[51]

The Five Points Artesian Well:

A water shortage is not a new phenomenon for Atlanta. In 1884, in order to address the city's inadequate water supply, the city council authorized the drilling of an artesian well at Five Points.[52] The well was 2,044 feet deep and provided 200,000 gallons of drinking water daily.[53] Water lines were connected to the well and installed along downtown streets with spigots installed at convenient points, each with an iron cup attached to a chain. Drinking from these communal cups, must have given pause to the hygiene-conscious early Atlantan.

At Least the Gold on the Gold Dome is From Georgia:

As part of the negotiations surrounding the relocation of the state Capitol from Milledgeville to Atlanta during Reconstruction, the City of Atlanta offered the State Legislature its choice of any ten-acre site in or around Atlanta or, alternatively, the five-acre City Hall lot downtown.[54] The city also promised to build "a Capitol building as good as the old Capitol building in Milledgeville."[55] The Legislature chose the City Hall lot and allowed the city to reimburse the Legislature $55,625.00, the value of the Milledgeville Capitol building, rather than requiring the city to construct the new Capitol building itself.[56] On November 1, 1880, the city conveyed the City Hall lot to the State of Georgia and in 1883, the Legislature appropriated $1,000,000 for the construction of the Capitol building.[57]

A miracle occurred on Capitol Avenue, as the construction of the Capitol was completed $118.43 under budget in 1889.[58] However, to cut cost and meet the budget, Indiana oolitic limestone was used instead of Georgia granite. Garrett cites *Harper's Weekly* of August 3, 1889 which provided "…so the Capitol was built of Indiana limestone, though Stone Mountain, only 15 miles away, raises its granite sides in sullen protest."[59] Georgia granite was used, however, in Washington, D.C. (where coming in under budget has historically been less important if not frowned upon) for the Thomas Jefferson Monument, the Arlington Memorial Bridge and in the Washington Monument.[60]

Haverty's Makes Its Home:

Haverty's furniture store has a long history in Atlanta. In 1885, 27 year-old James J. Haverty opened a small furniture store at 14 East Hunter Street with $600 of borrowed funds.[61] Interestingly, Haverty was "one of the few adult citizens of Atlanta in 1885 who bore the distinction of having been born in the city."[62] Prior to opening the store, Haverty had clerked in a dry goods store and been the manager of the carpet department at Rich & Bros., predecessor to Rich's, now known as Macy's.[63] Haverty and his brother, Micheal, operated the new furniture store until 1889, when J. J. Haverty and Amos G. Rhodes (founder of Rhodes Furniture) formed a partnership.[64] This partnership continued until 1908, at which time it was dissolved and Mr. Haverty formed the Haverty Furniture Company.[65]

Atlanta's Cyclorama Was Originally Displayed in the Motor City:

In October, 1885, a group of German artists, and the staff artist of *Harper's Weekly,* arrived in Atlanta to recon the area east of the city where the July 22, 1864, Battle of Atlanta was fought. The purpose of this field work was to assist them in the painting of a cyclorama.[66] The artists were employed by William Wehner, owner of the American Cyclorama Company of Milwaukee, Wisconsin.[67]

To insure the accuracy of the topography in their work, they constructed a 40-foot observation tower beside the Georgia Railroad at the approximate location of the intersection of the Georgia Railroad and Moreland Avenue.[68] Once their field work was completed, they returned to Milwaukee in the latter half of 1885 to start work on the project.[69] The painting, which was finished in 1886 or late 1887, "weighed 18,000 pounds; measured 50 feet in height and 400 feet in circumference, and cost $40,000."[70]

The cyclorama began its tour as a traveling exhibit in Detroit in February, 1887, then moved to Minneapolis. It was then sent to Indianapolis where it was housed in a specially-constructed circular building and then opened to the public in May, 1888.[71]

The enterprise went out of business, however. In September of 1890, the painting was auctioned off.[72] The painting was acquired for $2,500 by Paul M. Atkinson who brought the painting back to Atlanta in February, 1892, after a stint in Nashville and Chattanooga.[73]

When the cyclorama was moved to Atlanta, it took the place of another Wehner cyclorama illustrating the Civil War Battle of Missionary Ridge (outside Chattanooga, Tennessee) in a specially-constructed building on the north side of Edgewood Avenue between Courtland Street and Piedmont Avenue.[74] The Battle of Atlanta Cyclorama was placed on exhibit February 22, 1892.[75]

Due to diminishing patronage, after approximately 12 months, Atkinson sold the painting to H. H. Harrison of Florida who planned to put it on display at the 1893 World's Fair in Chicago.[76] But the city of Chicago required Harrison to build a brick building for the cyclorama which, because of cost, "caused the failure of the enterprise."[77] The painting hung in the Edgewood location until a snow storm collapsed the roof, seriously damaging the painting. Garrett writes that "[t]axes and rent accumulated and with the picture seriously damaged, Mr. Harrison abandoned it and it was sold [at auction] for expenses."[78] The auction was held on August 1, 1892, to satisfy a judgment of $937.35 which had accrued.[79] Ernest Woodruff purchased the painting for $1,100 and soon thereafter sold it to George V. Gress and Charles Northern who planned to move the painting to Grant Park.[80]

The painting was put on display in Grant Park in the fall of 1892.[81] In 1897, Gress offered to deed the painting to the City of Atlanta as a gift, conditioned upon the city's making general improvements to the building, including a new roof and repairing the damage to the painting.[82] The city accepted the conditions and took title to the cycloroama in 1898.[83] The painting remained in a circular wooden shingle building until 1921, when it was moved to the fireproof marble building where it remains to this day.[84] With W.P.A. (Works Progress Administration) funds, between 1934-1936, scenery and artifacts were added at the base of the painting to create a three-dimensional effect.[85] During 1979-1982, the painting was repaired and re-hung and the dirt in the foreground was replaced with fiberglass.[86] The painting measures 42 x 358 feet and is the largest oil painting in the world.[87]

"They're Healing Me With Science":

Christian Science was developed by Mrs. Mary Baker Eddy in 1879.[88] Christian Science arrived in Atlanta in 1886, with a Ms. Julia Bartlett who moved from Boston and began treating patients and teaching a Christian Science class.[89] A certain Mrs. Livingston Mims sought help from Bartlett for an illness that doctors had been unable to cure. Ms. Bartlett was able to heal Mrs. Mims, who, deeply moved by the experience, became an active believer in Christian Science.[90] Mrs. Mims began teaching Christian Science in her home and after a few months, rented a small room in a building on Peachtree Street where she began to hold regular Sunday services.[91] The church moved to a larger space on Broad Street. In January, 1896, it began holding services at the DeGive's Opera House (which later became the Loews Grand Theatre, the location of the 1939 movie premiere of "Gone With the Wind," and is now the site of the Georgia Pacific building at 133 Peachtree Street).[92]

The organization later built a church on the north side of Baker Street between West Peachtree and Spring streets.[93] In 1909, the church purchased a lot at 15th and Peachtree Street from Ernest Woodruff and built a new building which was completed in July, 1914.[94] The second Christian Science church was built at the corner of Peachtree and Stratford roads in Buckhead, the third at 850 Cascade Avenue, S.W. and a fourth at 427 Moreland Avenue, N.E.[95]

Fort McPherson Originally to be Named Fort Hancock:

Prior to 1880, the U.S. Army had constructed barracks, known as the McPherson Barracks, off Peters Street in Atlanta. The McPherson Barracks were named for General James McPherson, an Union Major General who was killed in action during the Battle of Atlanta on July 22, 1864.[96] The barracks were abandoned by the U.S. military in the early 1880's however.[97] In 1885, Congress appropriated $500,000 to build a post in the Atlanta vicinity.[98] General Winfield Scott Hancock, another distinguished (Civil War) general and unsuccessful Democratic candidate for president in 1880, was sent to Atlanta to select a site for the new post.[99] After viewing several tracts, he selected 140 acres on the Central Railroad and East Point wagon road, which was the nucleus of the present Fort McPherson.[100] The new post was to be named Fort Hancock in his honor. Prior to completion, however, it was decided to preserve General McPherson's name.[101] Fort McPherson was completed by the end of 1888.[102] The base was closed in September, 2011, and is being repurposed and redeveloped.

A Coke Is Born:

The iconic soft drink was born of the patent medicine era. Coca-Cola was touted as having medicinal value and curative powers. John Styth "Doc" Pemberton, the inventor of Coca-Cola syrup, was born in 1833, in Knoxville, Georgia and later moved to Columbus, Georgia.[103] After obtaining a temporary physician's degree at the Southern Botanico-Medical College in Macon, Georgia, he returned to Columbus and became a retail and wholesale druggist.[104]

In 1869, when Pemberton moved to Atlanta, he set up shop in the Kimball House for a period of time.[105] He subsequently became a member of

Pemberton, Wilson, Taylor & Company, wholesale druggists and manufacturing chemists at 23 and 25 Peachtree Street.[106] In January, 1886, Pemberton, Ed Holland, David D. Doe and Frank Mason Robinson incorporated Pemberton Chemical Company in a house owned by Ed Holland at 107 Marietta Street.[107] Pemberton had already been producing French Wine of Coca on his own and renting the house from Holland since the end of 1885.[108] The stated purpose of the new corporation was the manufacture of patent medicines.[109] Holland, formerly the landlord, turned over title to his house for a share in the business.[110] Doe and Robinson were to handle the printing of the ads and promotional side of the business.[111]

A little background on Robinson, Frank Mason Robinson was born in 1846 in East Corinth, Maine, and started merchandising with David Doe in Bangor, Maine. Robinson later moved to Sibley, Iowa, then came to Atlanta in 1885 with Doe, and a printing press, with the intent to start an advertising business.[112]

The story of the creation of the famous Coca-Cola syrup recipe is intertwined with the introduction of cocaine to America. America was introduced to the drug cocaine through President Ulysses S. Grant's unsuccessful battle with throat cancer.[113] Grant gained relief from the unbearable pain by taking cocaine, both topically and by ingestion.[114] Paris-based chemist Angelo Mariani supplied Grant with this new miracle drug, which had been introduced to him by Parisian doctor Charles Fauvel, a pioneer in using the drug as an anesthetic.[115] Also an entrepreneur, Mariani tried mixing the drug with tea and pate to create a marketable product.[116] He found success by mixing it with wine, creating Vin Mariani, which by the 1880's became a global enterprise.[117] Copying the recipe, Pemberton came up

23

with French Wine of Coca in Atlanta (not Columbus). Doc Pemberton copied Mariani's recipe and later told a reporter that he "followed very closely the most approved French formula," which "was available from the French Pharmaceutical Codex and other sources."[118] Pemberton did alter the recipe slightly by "adding in a pinch of another popular new drug, extract of the African Kola nut."[119]

Many believe, incorrectly, that Pemberton then developed Coca-Cola as a carbonated beverage due to prohibition ordinances enacted in Atlanta and Fulton County in or around 1886. Frederick Allen sets the record straight in *The Secret Formula*, explaining that the invention of Coca-Cola was driven by the fact that there was a larger market for cheap soft drinks, than for patent medicines. The following is an excerpt from page 26 of *The Secret Formula*:

> **There is a common misconception that Coca-Cola evolved from French Wine of Coca. The voters of Atlanta narrowly approved a referendum on November 2, 1885, calling for local prohibition, and it was scheduled to go into effect July 1, 1886. Some historians have speculated that Pemberton, checkmated at his moment of triumph by a law banning alcohol, retreated to the lab, removed the wine from French Wine of Coca, and emerged with a non-alcoholic substitute, Coca-Cola. It makes a tidy theory, but isn't true. The local law closed the saloons... but other liquor sales were unaffected.**
>
> **Actually, the impetus behind the development of Coca-Cola was a bit more mercenary. By 1886, Atlanta had five soda fountains operating during the summer months, and the principals of Pemberton Chemical wanted a beverage they could sell by the glass. At 75 cents or $1 a bottle, even the most popular patent medicines had a limited market and tended to appeal to those who were sick or thought they were. But almost everyone could afford a nickel for a soft drink, and the potential clientele**

included anyone who got thirsty during the frying-pan heat of Atlanta's summer season.[120]

It was Frank Mason Robinson who suggested Pemberton create this new product. It was also Robinson who came up with the name "Coca-Cola" after two of the new recipe's ingredients, the coca leaf and the kola nut, changing the "K" in Kola to a "C" for the sake of uniformity.[121] Robinson is also credited with designing the flowing script lettering for the famous trademark.

With regard to the actual creation of the recipe, in keeping with the stated purpose of Pemberton Chemical Company, Coca-Cola was originally sold as a syrup to be mixed with soda water as a medicinal product. Pemberton claimed it cured morphine addition, dyspepsia, neurasthenia, headache and impotence.[122] Pemberton's choice of ingredients was avant-garde, as well as practical, and the process included some trial and error. At about the same time as European doctors were discovering the medicinal effects of cocaine, they were also discovering and experimenting with the seed of the Kola fruit, which became available commercially in 1881.[123] The Kola seed's active ingredient was caffeine. Pemberton began concocting recipes with the extract of Kola as its base; however, the extract of Kola is extremely bitter.[124] Pemberton turned to synthetic, powdered Kola which was less bitter.[125] Pemberton then solved the bitterness problem by adding burnt sugar which at the time was known as caramel.[126] It was this caramel that gave the syrup concoction its "dark, distinctive, port-wine color."[127] Allen writes "[c]aramel in the form of burnt sugar . . . was widely used as a coloring agent in patent medicines. ... [and] [a]mong other things, it helped conceal any foreign matter that might fall, crawl or fly into the vat during preparation."[128]

The coca extract was not seemingly the primary ingredient, in fact, "Pemberton added to this brew the fluid extract of coca leaves."[129]

Once in a While You Get Shown the Light in the Strangest of Places if You Look at it Right:

According to legend, the creation of Coca-Cola, the carbonated beverage, happened by chance circumstance. In this version, a customer whose name was not recorded, walked into Jacob's Drug Store at Five Points with a headache and asked Willis E. Venable, operator of the soda fountain, for a bottle of Coca-Cola. Jacob's Drug Store was located at the site of the former Wachovia Bank of Georgia Building at Five Points which is now owned by the U.S. Government and used for offices.

The customer asked Venable to open it for him, add water, and let him take it there "to hasten relief."[130] The shelf containing the Coca-Cola syrup bottles was purportedly closer to the soda fountain than the sink and there happened to be a clean glass already at the soda fountain. For his own convenience, Venable suggested soda water rather than tap water.[131] According to Garrett, "[w]hen the customer drank the bubbling dose he enthusiastically proclaimed that it really tasted fine."[132] The word spread among the few druggists who stocked Coca-Cola syrup and they started serving it this way for customers who had a headache.[133] The legend was incorrect however; according to *The Secret Formula*, "[t]he plan from the very outset was to squirt it into a glass and spritz it with cold, carbonated water from the fountain."[134]

Coca-Cola, B.C.:

Pemberton believed in the future of Coca-Cola but he lacked the cash and the state of health to effectively market the product.[135] In a move which could be described as not completely forthright, Pemberton had obtained the trademark for "Cola-Cola Syrup and Extract" in his own name, not Pemberton Chemical Company.[136] In the summer of 1887, Pemberton offered to sell 2/3 of the rights to Coca-Cola to his friend George S. Lowndes. Pemberton wanted to retain 1/3 for his son, Charles M. Pemberton.[137] Lowndes originally turned the offer down due to other business interests, but reconsidered when Pemberton suggested he get a partner to handle the day-to-day operations of the company.[138] Lowndes partnered with Willis E. Venable, referenced above, who was "the leading soda fountain man in Atlanta, and at the time, chief local purveyor of Coca-Cola."[139]

On July 8, 1887, Lowndes and Venable bought Pemberton's 2/3 interest for $1,200 along with the right to manufacture and sell Coca-Cola. The equipment to produce Coca-Cola was then moved from 107 Marietta Street to the basement of Jacob's Drug Store.[140] According to Allen, "[t]he partners in Pemberton Chemical were completely left out" since Pemberton had obtained the trademark in his own name.[141] Pemberton sold the rights a second time to four more businessmen.[142] According to one source, by 1888, there were three versions of Coca-Cola on the market, one sold by Candler, one by the four businessmen, and one by Pemberton's son.[143]

Although the plan was for Venable to run the company, Venable was too busy running his drugstore to devote time to the production of Coca-Cola in his basement.[144] Venable did not make a single drop of new syrup.[145] Lowndes accordingly became apprehensive about the partnership and bought out Venable.[146] Lowndes quickly found that he also was too busy to promote the company and sought a buyer for his 2/3 interest.[147] Woolfold Walker, a former salesman for Pemberton Chemical Company, and his sister, Mrs. M. C. Dozier, purchased Lowndes' 2/3 interest on December 14, 1887 for $1,200.[148] Walker did not have any money to contribute, but convinced his younger sister to use $1,200 she and her husband obtained from the sale of their house in Columbus, Georgia. She initially refused because they needed the funds for a house in Atlanta, but ultimately agreed.[149] The manufacturing equipment was then transported back to 107 Marietta Street.[150]

Fish Don't Fry in the Kitchen, Beans Don't Burn on the Grill:

Although born into a cultured and distinguished family in Villa Rica, Georgia, Asa Griggs Candler arrived in Atlanta on July 7, 1873 "with exactly $1.75 in his pockets."[151] Candler was born in 1851, the eighth child of Samuel Charles Candler and Martha Beall Chandler; his father was a "planter, miner, developer and merchant in Villa Rica."[152] Candler spent his first day in Atlanta looking for work and even stopped by Doc Pemberton's store in the Kimball House lobby to ask for employment, which he was denied.[153] Candler had apprenticed with two doctors in Cartersville, Georgia, and was able to obtain a menial job from pharmacist George J. Howard at the very end of that first day in Atlanta.[154] For a period of time, Candler slept on a cot in the basement of Howard's store at 47 Peachtree Street.[155] Candler fell in love with, and married, Howard's daughter. Howard did not originally approve of either action.[156] Candler started his own business in 1877, but after Howard offered to "bury the hatchet," went into business again with this father-in-law.[157]

Frank M. Robinson (mentioned previously) pitched the idea of buying Doc Pemberton's remaining 1/3 interest in Coca-Cola to Asa Candler during the winter of 1888.[158] It was not until Candler tried Coca-Cola in an effort to cure his recurring headaches and dyspepsia that Candler became interested.[159] Walker, Candler and Company was thus formed and bought Pemberton's remaining 1/3 interest on April 14, 1888, for $550.[160]

Three days later, on April 17, 1888, Candler bought half the interests of Dozier and Walker (*i.e.*, 1/3 of the company) for $750.[161] This gave Candler a 1/3 interest plus the 1/9 interest he acquired when Pemberton was bought out.[162] On August 30, 1888, Candler purchased the remaining 1/3 interest of Walker and Dozier for $1,000.[163] On April 22, 1891, he acquired all of Walker, Candler and Company's 1/3 interest (formerly the 1/3 interest of Pemberton).[164] Candler's total outlay for all of the Coca-Cola shares was $2,300.[165]

Candler believed the formula needed some tweaking to "insure its uniformity and stability," and employed Frank M. Robinson to make these changes.[166]

Candler expanded quickly and by 1890 syrup sales had reached 9,000 gallons per year.[167]

Candler needed a substantial injection of capital to meet demand, so he decided to incorporate and sell shares. On January 29, 1892, The Coca-Cola Company was chartered as a Georgia corporation.[168] The corporation issued 1,000 shares at $100 a share. Candler kept 500, gave Frank M. Robinson 10 and offered 490 through stockbrokers in Boston, New York and other cities.[169] Only 75 shares were purchased; the buyer was F. W. Prescott, a broker in Boston.[170] However, the lack of interest in the IPO did not slow the company's progress. By 1904, sales had reached 1 million gallons annually, and by 1911, Coca-Cola was spending $1 million annually on advertising.[171] In 1916, the distinctive bottle was designed and patented.[172] By 1908, "the company was regularly netting profits of $2 million and $3 million a year, making Candler the richest man in Atlanta."[173] Little boys would say, "who do you think I am? Asa G. Candler?" as they spurned their friends' requests to borrow a dime or quarter."[174] However, according to *The Secret Formula*, Candler "took little satisfaction from his fabulous financial success. . . [and] "had a sort of Old Testament ferocity about the temptations of wealth."[175] Candler's take on money was that it "ought to be properly earned and usefully spent, and it was plain that the profits pouring in from Coca-Cola bothered him on both counts."[176] When Candler's accumulation of wealth became almost automatic, it "seemed to scratch a raw spot on his conscience."[177]

Asa Candler officially turned over the reins when the Coca-Cola Company was purchased on September 12, 1919 for $25,000,000, by a syndicate led by The Trust Company of Georgia (now SunTrust), which was masterminded by Ernest Woodruff.[178] Asa Candler had turned over most of his shares to his five children in the previous couple of years.[179] Charles Howard Candler, Asa G. Candler, Jr., Walter T. Candler, William Candler, Mrs. Henry C. Heinz along with Judge John S. Candler, Samuel C. Dobbs, Frank M. Robinson and Samuel L. Willard were the majority shareholders at the time of the sale.[180] 500,000 shares of stock in the new company were issued in the public offering at $40.00 per share.[181]

Is There Cocaine in it?

By the end of the 1890's, syrup sales had reached 281,000 gallons. Often customers would ask for "a shot in the arm" or a "Dope" or a "Coke."[182]

Candler wanted to know if there was still any active cocaine (and not just flavoring) in his product as a result of the use of coca extract. In the summer of 1891, Candler shipped a quart of Coca-Cola to LaGrange, Georgia, to be tested by Dr. H. R. Slack, the president of the Georgia Pharmaceutical Association and chemical examiner for the Georgia State Board of Pharmacy.[183]

Slack concluded that it *did* have cocaine in it, but said "the quantity of cocaine is so small that it would be simply impossible for anyone to form the cocaine habit from drinking Coca-Cola, for it would require about thirty glasses, as usually drawn from the fount, to make an ordinary dose of the drug."[184] Candler thought he and Frank Robinson had removed the cocaine or left only a miniscule, "undetectable trace" when they changed the formula three years prior.[185] An "ordinary dose" of cocaine was defined generally at that time as one full grain.[186] Candler was behind the eight ball. He could not remove the fluid extract of the coca leaves completely, because he believed that "he must have at least some by-product of the coca leaf in the syrup (along with some kola) to protect his right to the name Coca-Cola."[187] And since Candler only had rights to the name, and did not have a patent on the syrup, he believed it was imperative to protect the name.

Candler and Robinson went back to work to modify the formula, putting the coca leaves and kola nuts through a "rigorous treatment process to remove practically all of the active properties."[188] But even though Candler was intent on removing the cocaine, he could not let go of advertising Coca-Cola as a drink with amazing curative properties. According to Allen in *The Secret Formula*, "Candler could never bring himself to abandon the suggestive, overblown language of the earliest promotion for coca and kola as patent medicines."[189] Candler wanted it both ways: "[t]here was no flat denial, no categorical statement that Coca-Cola was free from cocaine, and no retreat from the carnival barker's spiel."[190]

But the advertising of Coca-Cola as a drink with medicinal qualities got Candler more than he bargained for when it caught the attention of the U.S. government. Congress passed a stamp tax on medicines to help finance the Spanish-American War in 1898. The IRS ordered Coca-Cola to pay the tax citing "the health claims of the company's advertising."[191] Candler paid the tax under protest but sued the U.S. government to get the money back. Interestingly, in preparing for the trial, the government's chemist could not detect any cocaine in Coca-Cola. Coca-Cola's chemist, using more sophisticated equipment than the government had access to, did find "one 400th of a grain of cocaine per ounce."[192] It was such a minute amount that the Coca-Cola chemist thought it would take "a hundred glasses of Coca-Cola before a consumer could feel any effect from the cocaine."[193] At the trial, the government's chemist, a Dr. Crampton, did testify that there was a small amount of cocaine in Coca-Cola, and implied - but never actually said - that his tongue was numbed by it.[194] But this testimony "quickly disintegrated into a hodge podge of fragmentary answers," and Dr. Crampton then "abruptly left the stand dismissed by both sides."[195]

The jury (of Georgians) found in favor of Coca-Cola, but Dr. Crampton's testimony was later cited incorrectly in a U.S. Supreme Court opinion written by Oliver Wendell Holmes which fanned the flames of the rumors that Coca-Cola did contain an appreciable amount of cocaine.[196] According to *The Secret Formula*, "Dr. Crampton's testimony was misremembered as convincing evidence that Coca-Cola once contained enough cocaine to numb a man's tongue, and the vivid notion quickly found its way into the public consciousness and later into the history books."[197] The Coca-Cola Company still to this day promotes the mystique of the secret formula.

Not long after the trial, Candler became determined to eliminate unequivocally every last trace of cocaine in Coca-Cola, not because of the trial, but because of the public's increasingly fearful attitude toward cocaine. Around 1900, a scare started to spread throughout the South about cocaine and "the trigger was race."[198] Local prohibition laws were put on the books throughout the South, and "in some instances blacks - like other poor people who could not afford bootleg liquor - turned to cocaine as a substitute."[199] In 1900, the *Journal of The American Medical Association* reported that African-Americans in the South "were becoming addicted to sniffing cocaine."[200] Rumors and fear started to spread. Across the country, ordinances and statutes were passed restricting the use of cocaine in patent medicines. There was a backlash against kola also.[201]

To completely eliminate cocaine from Coca-Cola, Candler sought the help of Roessler & Hasslacher Chemical Company, oddly enough, the largest legal cocaine manufacturer in the United States.[202] Candler met with Dr. Louis Schaefer at the chemical company who believed he could remove all the cocaine. Schaefer developed an exhaustive chemical process that did, in fact, remove all the cocaine.[203] And, in 1907, the USDA tested Coca-Cola for that purpose and confirmed conclusively "that Coca-Cola syrup no longer had any cocaine in it."[204]

Coca-Cola Bottling; Candler Did Indeed Give Away the Rights:

During the summer of 1899, two young attorneys from Chattanooga, Tennessee, Benjamin Franklin Thomas and Joseph Brown Whitehead, visited Asa Candler.[205]

Thomas had served in the U.S. Army's commissary department in Cuba during the Spanish-American War and had noted that a carbonated drink similar to Coca-Cola had sold very well.[206] When he returned home, he shared the idea of bottling Coca-Cola with his friend Joseph Brown Whitehead, which prompted the visit to Candler.

Candler's response was "tepid," according to Garrett.[207] First of all, he was already selling approximately 30,000 gallons a year. Secondly, he had already given Joseph Beiden Ham, a retailer in Vicksburg, Mississippi, verbal permission to bottle and sell Coca-Cola in and around the Vicksburg area.[208]

Thomas and Whitehead assured Candler that they would assume complete responsibility for other bottling operations. Candler granted Thomas and Whitehead the right to bottle and distribute Coca-Cola as a carbonated beverage throughout most of the United States *for free*.[209] The six New England states were initially held out of the transaction since Candler's fountain wholesaler had a dormant bottling option there.[210] Thomas and Whitehead returned to their hotel and expeditiously drafted a 600-word contract which was executed on July 21, 1889.[211] Candler told them that, if they failed, not to "come back and cry on [his] shoulder because [he had] very little confidence in this bottling business."[212] The enterprise was not without its challenges. Bottles would sometimes explode because of the carbonation. The bottle used originally was the Hutchinson bottle which was sealed by a rubber gasket.[213] According to *The Secret Formula*, "[s]oda pop got its nickname from the "pop" that resulted when the wire and stopper were pushed down into the bottle."[214] The bottles were difficult to clean and sterilize. Fortunately for the struggling bottlers, a Baltimore mechanical engineer named William Painter patented the bottle cap around 1900.[215] This made the Hutchinson bottle obsolete and allowed for "striking advances in mechanized washing and sterilization."[216] Sales rose dramatically and by 1909, there were 397 bottling plants in the U.S.[217] According to *The Secret Formula*, "[i]n most cities, a franchise to bottle Coca-Cola was now considered a license to make money."[218]

By 1900, Thomas and Whitehead realized that it would make sense to divide their territory.[219] By mutual consent, Thomas remained in Chattanooga and took the "northern territory" and Whitehead took the "southern territory."[220] Whitehead moved to Atlanta and opened a bottling plant on the east side of Ivy Street between Decatur and Gilmer streets.[221] Whitehead and Thomas determined that the only way to make the bottling business work was to "sub-franchise" out the bottling rights to "sub-bottlers" who would build the actual bottling facilities and sell the product in their "sub-franchised" areas.[222] Whitehead and Thomas thus became the "parent" bottlers (i.e., the middlemen) and made vast sums of money.

The Coca-Cola Bottle: Cacao is It!

Veazey Rainwater became the head of Whitehead's southern parent bottling company after Whitehead died of pneumonia at the age of 42.[223] Harold Hirsh, Coca-Cola's general counsel, and Rainwater spearheaded the project to design a distinctive bottle for Coca-Cola because the current, nondistinct bottle, was causing several issues.[224] Bottled Coca-Cola was typically sold at the time in large tubs of ice along with other bottled soft drinks.[225] Customers would reach into the tub for a drink without knowing which brand they were grabbing.[226] Even when they pulled the bottle out, since the glued-on label had usually come off in the cooler ice-water, the customer still did not know the brand he had chosen.[227] All of the bottles were the same: ordinary-shaped, straight-sided bottles.

Rainwater and Hirsch realized that putting Coca-Cola in a distinctive bottle would help enormously with marketing, and a trademarked package would help Hirsch in his legal battles with Coca-Cola's competitors.[228] Using a slightly smaller bottle, six to six and a half ounces, would help profits too.[229]

In the summer of 1913, the Root Glass Company of Terre Haute, Indiana, one of Coca-Cola's bottle suppliers, was shut down due to a heat wave.[230] With free time on his hands, plant manager Alex Samuelson started tinkering with ideas for a new bottle.[231] One idea was to incorporate the shape or the characteristics of some of the original ingredients of Coca-Cola.[232] Pursuing this, he sent an employee, Clyde Edwards, to the city library to look up information on the kola seed and coca leaves.[233] Edwards, however, "ended up on the wrong page of Encyclopedia Britannica."[234] Samuelson and Edwards created a bottle design "whose vertical striations and curved, bulging middle have no resemblance whatsoever of the coca leaf or the kola nut, but instead was a dead ringer for the totally unrelated seed pod of the cacao tree, the source of chocolate."[235] Rainwater loved the design and was completely unaware of the research error.[236] The new bottle was adopted after a few technical changes and C. J. Root, who held the patent, was offered a royalty of 25 cents per gross on all bottles manufactured with the new design.[237] Root took 5 cents per gross "and ended up the wealthiest man in Indiana anyway."[238]

Keeping Track: The History of Piedmont Park:

A certain Joseph Kingsbury conceived the idea of starting a club and exposition area in Atlanta. According to Garrett, "[s]ince the close of the Exposition of 1881, and the occupancy by the Exposition Mills of the old Oglethorpe Park with its track, Kingsbury and his friends lacked a satisfactory place to ride [horses]"[239] Kingsbury and his colleagues decided to organize a private club and convinced 100 men to pledge $100 each towards the endeavor.[240] Kingsbury conducted a meeting on January 4, 1887, to organize a Driving Association and discuss the purchase of a location.[241] Famed *Atlanta Constitution* managing editor Henry Grady attended and promoted the idea that, if a suitable property could be obtained for a riding track, it could also be used for an annual fair.[242] The club considered several sites including a tract across from Fort McPherson, the George W. Collier tract (described in further detail subsequently), which comprised approximately what is now the Ansley Park Golf Club and course, and the Henry L. Wilson tract, which is now the Orme Circle neighborhood adjacent to Piedmont Park.[243] All met the acreage requirement for a 1 mile race track.[244]

On March 21, 1887, the Collier property was selected, but Collier "pulled the plug by insisting upon certain terms to which the Driving Club committee would not agree."[245]

The Gentlemen's Driving Club approached Benjamin F. Walker about selling his land (a tract not originally considered) for the driving park. Walker's father had built a homestead on the property overlooking Clear Creek years earlier and had deeded it to his son.[246]

Walker agreed to sell his 189.43 acre tract, and on July 1, 1887, delivered a warranty deed for the land which is now Piedmont Park to the Gentleman's Driving Club for the price of $38,000.[247] The club's ballroom sits on what was once the backyard of the Walker home.[248]

The entire acreage secured from Mr. Walker was purchased by the Gentleman's Driving Club. Two years later, the Piedmont Exposition Company purchased the tract from the club for the purpose of producing expositions at the site. The club retained the portion of the tract which makes up its present grounds.[249] The first Piedmont Exposition was held on the grounds in October, 1887, and drew 20,000 visitors.[250] Charles Collier (George Washington Collier's nephew) was a major investor, and helped produce the first Piedmont Exposition, the 1895 Cotton States Exposition and the intervening expositions leading up to 1895 exposition.[251] The main purpose of the Piedmont Expositions was to showcase the mutual resources of the Piedmont region including Georgia, North Carolina, South Carolina, Tennessee and Alabama.[252] The site quickly became known as "Piedmont Park" and Piedmont Avenue was so named for the same reason.[253] The

Piedmont Expositions set the stage for the 1895 Cotton States and International Exposition.

As mentioned above, the Piedmont Exposition Company purchased the entire property from the Gentleman's Driving Club on February 20, 1889.[254] The terms of the deal required the Piedmont Exposition Company to pay off $60,000 of the Gentleman's Driving Club's debts and give the Gentleman's Driving Club $28,500 of common stock of the Piedmont Exposition Company.[255] After the sale, the Piedmont Exposition Company set aside the grounds, substantially as now occupied by the Piedmont Driving Club, for "use by such shareholders of the Exposition Company as would pay annual dues and the Gentlemen's Driving Club continued to function as before."[256]

When the Cotton States and International Exposition of 1895 began to materialize, a new charter was obtained for the Gentleman's Driving Club and the name was changed to the Piedmont Driving Club as part of that process on November 20, 1895.[257]

After the Cotton States Exposition of 1895, there was discussion about using the property for a cotton mill.[258] As a result, a group of investors was formed to purchase the stock of the Piedmont Exposition Company and prevent this from happening.[259] Around the same time, the city of Atlanta began to express an interest in the property (which at the time was outside the city limits) for holding annual expositions. The investors decided to offer the park to the city.

On May 23, 1904, the City Council took up two very important resolutions in a special session. The first was to extend the city limits to the north to include most of the area now comprising Piedmont Park.²⁶⁰ The second was to actually purchase Piedmont Park (consisting of 185 acres) from the Piedmont Park Exposition Company for $99,000.00.²⁶¹ There was no opposition to the city limit extension but there was "a sharp debate [which] developed on the proposal to purchase the park."²⁶² Councilman Fletcher A. Quilman, was of the opinion "that Piedmont Park was not fitted for park purposes," because it was just an open field.²⁶³ Fortunately, the resolution passed 9-to-2 and the sale was consummated on Monday, June 20, 1904.²⁶⁴ The city purchased the park for "$38,000 cash and assumed debt of $60,000 in bonds which it paid off."²⁶⁵ In May, 1904, the city limits were extended to include the park.²⁶⁶ On November 5, 1907, the city sold the Piedmont Driving Club "certain rights in part of Piedmont Park adjacent to the club grounds for $5,000," so the total outlay was $93,000.²⁶⁷

Tech Talk: The Origins of Georgia Tech:

In May, 1882, while sharing a walk, Major John Fletcher Hanson, who became the president of the Central of Georgia Railroad, and Nathaniel Edwin Harris, who became a representative in the State Legislature and later the Governor of Georgia, discussed the need for a technological school in Georgia.²⁶⁸ Harris remarked that "he would rather be the author of a law establishing such a school than to be a Governor of Georgia."²⁶⁹ Hanson responded that he should do exactly that.²⁷⁰ Taking Hanson's advice, Harris ran for the Legislature on this issue and won.²⁷¹ On November 24, 1882, he introduced a resolution authorizing the appointment of a committee to explore the issue.²⁷² A bill introduced to create the school was defeated due to the fact that the State would have to borrow the funds for the project. Because of the immense public debt incurred during Reconstruction, drafters of the

Constitution of 1877 "made it difficult [for the state] to incur debt for education or almost anything else."[273] Bob Toombs, one of the drafters, was quoted as saying, "We have locked the door of the Treasury and have thrown the key away."[274]

The creation of a technological school became one of the chief issues in the next legislative election.[275] Harris reintroduced the bill on October 15, 1885 and it passed.[276] Athens, Atlanta, Macon, Milledgeville and Penfield made a pitch for the school but Atlanta was chosen.[277] Garrett writes that many prominent Atlantans had contributed to a fund for the school.[278] The original Academic Building which is still standing and one of the most recognizable if not iconic buildings on the Georgia Tech campus, was built in 1888.[279]

The Academic Building, built in 1888, still stands today. The Shop Building, which stood next to it, and was of the same John Ruskin design, was destroyed by fire in 1892.

A ceremony was held for the opening of the school at De Give's Opera House on October 7, 1888.[280] The school was renamed Georgia Institute of Technology in 1949.[281] Georgia Tech's football field was donated by John W. Grant, a prominent Atlanta merchant who gave the funds in memory of his deceased son Hugh Inman Grant. Specifically, Garrett writes, it was Grant "who made possible the purchase of the tract."[282] It is the oldest continuously used on-campus site for college football in the southern United States, football having been played there since 1905.[283] The stadium was renamed Bobby Dodd Stadium in 1988 in honor of Bobby Dodd, the school's all-time winningest coach.[284] The playing surface is still called Grant Field.[285] Connecting the dots, John W. Grant built and resided at an estate located at 155 West Paces Ferry Road which is now the Cherokee Town Club.

The First Atlanta Zoo Was a Real Circus:

The Atlanta Zoo was opened at Grant Park in the spring of 1889, the result of a gift by lumber magnate George V. Gress.[286] As mentioned previously, Gress later donated the cyclorama to city, which is also located at Grant Park.[287] On March 28, 1889, Gress and Thomas J. James, a railroad contractor and lumberman, attended the auction of a defunct circus at the Fulton County courthouse.[288] After intense bidding, the circus was sold to Gress and James for $4,485. James was interested in the wagons and railroad cars for his business.[289] A few days later, Gress offered the animals to the city and thus began Atlanta's first municipal zoo. According to Garrett, the collection included "one hyena, two African lionesses, two silver lions, one black bear, two wildcats, one jaguar, one gazelle, one coon, one elk, one Mexican hog, two deer, one camel, one dromedary, two monkeys, two serpents - all with cages and carriages complete."[290]

What Fertilizer, Florida and Yellow Fever Have to do with Agnes Scott College:

George W. Scott was born in Alexandria, Pennsylvania in 1829.[291] In 1850, Scott moved to Tallahassee, Florida and made a fortune in cotton and merchandising.[292] He was a colonel of cavalry in the Confederate Army and, in 1868, was elected the governor of Florida.[293] In 1870, he moved to Savannah, and then to Decatur after the Savannah yellow fever epidemic of 1878.[294] In Decatur, he started a successful commercial fertilizer manufacturing company.[295] In December, 1888, a Reverend F. H. Gaines became the pastor of the Decatur Presbyterian Church, of which Scott was a member.[296] In the summer of 1889, Gaines began promoting the idea of "establishing a high school for girls under the auspices of the Presbyterian Church."[297] Colonel Scott was inspired.

Scott became one of the largest contributors for the new school and chaired the committee to acquire a site for the school.[298] The school rented a three-story residence in Decatur, known as the "White House," which faced the Georgia Railroad.[299] Originally named The Decatur Female Seminary, the school opened on September 24, 1889 with 60 students, three of which were boarders.[300] The "White House" was used until 1952, when it was torn down.[301] In 1890, Scott pledged $40,000 to secure a permanent location for the school.[302] Scott paid for the construction of the "Main Hall" which was dedicated on November 12, 1891.[303] In recognition of his generosity, the school's name was then changed to Agnes Scott Institute in honor of Colonel Scott's mother.[304]

The code of conduct was strict during the early years of the school. Garrett cites an 1892 school bulletin which provides:

> The following violations of the laws of health are prohibited: Eating imprudently at night; wearing thin shoes in cold weather; sitting on the ground or going outdoors with uncovered heads; too early removal of flannels or neglect to put them on at the approach of cold weather. No pupil is allowed to appear in a wrapper outside of her own chamber. Pupils will not be allowed to go to Atlanta oftener than once a quarter for shopping purposes. No one will be excused from breakfast except in the case of illness. Visitors will not be received during school or study hours, nor the visits of young men at any time. Pupils are permitted to correspond only with such gentlemen as are specially named in writing by parents.[305]

Word on the street is that some, if not all, of these rules have been relaxed at present-day Agnes Scott College.

Contrary to What We Told the IOC, Atlanta Does Need One of These: Atlanta's First Sewer System:

Before 1880, there was no sewer system in Atlanta. Some of the higher-end homeowners installed sewer pipes to the main headstream of the South River that "came from a spring under the Kimball House and ran in a southerly direction along Loyd (now Central Avenue) Street to Fair Street."[306] Around 1880, the city lined the stream with rocks and covered it, which constituted Atlanta's first rudimentary sewer.[307] In 1885, the city engaged Rudolph Hering to perform a study of the sewer needs of the growing city.[308] Taken from the out-of-sight, out-of-mind school of sewer design, Hering's plan was a sewer system that would carry the sewerage outside the city and dump it into five brooks flowing away from town.[309] It was an improvement, but "contaminated every stream in the vicinity, including the South River, the site of Atlanta's Water Works, which soon had to be moved to the Chattahoochee River."[310] The Hering sewerage system was completed in

1890, but outhouses still outnumbered indoor plumbing by 3 to 1.[311] Garrett writes that "[t]welve two-horse night-soil wagons were kept busy during 1889 hauling 7,112 loads of human excrement to the dumping grounds west of the city," proving unequivocally that there are worse jobs than practicing insurance defense law.[312]

Atlanta outgrew the 1890 sewer very quickly. In 1910, Hering was engaged to prepare a second study.[313] The 1910 plan, slightly more environmentally friendly, recommended "trunk-line sewers far down the major creek valleys to treatment plants where the sewage could be treated in Imhoff Tanks."[314] Garrett explains in a footnote that these tanks, invented by Dr. Karl Imhoff, consisted of a two story septic tank.[315] One of the plants was (and is) located on Peachtree Creek at the mouth of Tanyard Branch which is now part of Bobby Jones Golf Course.[316] The Imhoff Tanks, which were completed in 1912, were the first large Imhoff Tanks in the U.S.[317] A smaller Imhoff Tank had been installed in 1911 in New Jersey.[318] The Clayton Plant, a well known sewer treatment plant on Atlanta Road, was built during the Depression with W.P.A. funds.[319]

College Park: A Lot for a Name:

College Park was originally incorporated as the city of Manchester in October 5, 1891.[320] The city's springs were touted as one of its most desirable features.[321] The *Atlanta Constitution* stated "[t]he elevation is six feet higher than that of Atlanta, and there are five or six splendid springs that gurgle continuous streams of pure cold water. One of these springs spurts a strong stream of chalybeate water, which is an attractive and desirable feature of the new town."[322] The name change to College Park arose from the relocation of Cox Female College (also known as the Cox College and Conservancy) from

La Grange, Georgia, to Manchester during the early 1890's. After considerable discussion, the name of the town was changed to College Park by act of the legislature on December 16, 1895, to be descriptive of the fact that the city was the location of an institution of higher learning.[323] The new name was actually the winning entry in a naming contest held by the city.[324] A certain Lula Roper submitted the winning name and won a "choice lot" in the city as a prize.[325]

The change to "College Park" freed up the name "Manchester" to be used for a city incorporated January 1, 1909 in Meriwether and Talbot Counties. The *new* Manchester is the birthplace of author Stewart Woods, who based his first book *Chiefs*, in Manchester, though he called in Delano in the book.

Cox College closed in 1923, reopened, then closed for good in 1938.[326] The school property was sold to the City of College Park and the Fulton County Board of Education. Currently, College Park City Hall, the city auditorium, the public library, McClarin High School and Woodward Academy are all located on the former Cox College Property.[327]

Passing Grady:

The Henry Grady Monument was unveiled on October 21, 1891. Henry Grady was known as the "Spokesman of the New South," and was the managing editor of The *Atlanta Constitution* in the 1880's.[328] The bronze statue was designed by Alexander Doyle of New York and cast at the Ames Foundry in Chicopee, Massachusetts.[329] The base of the monument is made of Georgia granite. Some 25,000 gathered for the unveiling.[330]

Grady Hospital, also named for Henry Grady was opened in May, 1892.³³¹ At a cost of approximately $105,000.00, its original capacity was 100 beds with ten of these for paying patients.³³²

Unveiled on October 21, 1891, the Henry Grady Monument located at the intersection of Marietta and Forsyth streets has stood the test of time.

The Craigie House:

The Atlanta Chapter of the Daughters of the American Revolution ("DAR") is the second oldest in the national society, the first chapter in Georgia, and the first chapter nationwide to own its own property.³³³ Incidentally, the Daughters of the American Revolution came into being because the Sons of the American Revolution, deciding they had had enough of the women-folk in the organization, voted to exclude women from membership in 1890.³³⁴ The first location of the Georgia chapter was the former Massachusetts building at the Cotton States and International Exposition of 1895.³³⁵ The Massachusetts building was an exact copy of the Craigie House in Cambridge, Massachusetts, that had served as Washington's first headquarters in the Revolutionary War. Later, it was Henry Wadsworth Longfellow's home.

The original Craigie House in Cambridge, Massachusetts was built in 1759 for John Vassell, who had to abandon it during the Revolutionary War because he was a loyalist.[336] Andrew Craigie, Washington's apothecary general, was the home's next owner.[337] For financial reasons, Craigie's widow, Elizabeth, starting taking in boarders. Longfellow was originally a boarder, but later became the owner as the result of a wedding gift from his father-in-law.[338]

The copy of the Massachusetts Craigie House constructed at Piedmont Park for the Exposition was donated to the Georgia DAR chapter in 1895 after the exposition ended. In October, 1895, in a ceremony before Mayor Porter King, the chairman of the Massachusetts Board of Managers for the exposition, presented the building to the City of Atlanta to be held in trust until the Atlanta DAR Chapter could obtain its charter.[339] The Georgia Chapter obtained permission from the Piedmont Exposition Company to allow the structure to remain at Piedmont Park until they could have the structure moved to its new location.[340]

George Washington Collier donated a lot across from Piedmont Park for the building in February, 1896.[341] Benjamin Walker also donated a small parcel to the east of the Collier lot so the lot would have access to Piedmont Avenue.[342] According to a newspaper account, the Collier gift also provided for a 25-foot wide strip of land for a road leading from the chapter house directly to Peachtree.[343] The new street was never built, however.

Both deeds, however, contained a right of reversion, which many deeds of gift do. The right of reversion provided that if the property ever ceased to be used for the chapter house, the property would revert to Collier and Walker, or their heirs. Determining that they would never be able to sell the property, the chapter did not accept the gift.[344] The costs of relocating the building ended up being more than the chapter expected. According to Tommy H. Jones, who has written extensively on the subject, "[i]t is possible, too, that the building was something less than the "permanent" structure that the donors claimed; and other problems with the building, besides the absence of heat, must have forced the decision that it would be better to build anew rather than move the building as originally planned."[345]

Fundraising for the construction of the new building started in 1903, "perhaps in anticipation of the city's purchase of Piedmont Park from the Piedmont Exposition Company in 1904."[346] Since 1896, when the Collier and Walker deeds were offered, Collier had died and the entire land lot, including the lot offered to the chapter, had been purchased by the Southern Real Estate Improvement Company (which was planning to develop Ansley Park). The Collier deed resurfaced in the process, and the Southern Real Estate Improvement Company again offered the lot to the chapter, this time without the reversion clause.[347] The heir of Benjamin Walker, Mrs. Lola A. (Frank) Clement, was unwilling to give the chapter the 30-foot strip to connect the lot to Piedmont Avenue that her father had offered in 1896.[348] In December, 1905, the chapter and Mrs. Clement negotiated a swap for 30 feet on the north side of the lot for Clement's 30 feet needed to connect to Piedmont.[349] With this, the chapter had complete title to the present site.

The Massachusetts building at Piedmont Park was sold for materials and torn down by 1909. Windows, doors and "some brick and boards" were retained and moved across the street to the new lot, but "it is not clear if any of that material was reused in constructing the present building."[350] Architect

Thomas Morgan was involved in the design of the new building. Morgan also designed North Avenue Presbyterian Church and the Healy Building.[351] Although fundraising was slow, the chapter applied for a building permit on October 7, 1910.[352] Samuel Venable, who owned part of Stone Mountain, donated the granite cornerstone for the chapter house, which formally opened on June 14, 1911.[353] In the 1920's, Arthur Murray rented the space periodically for dance instruction.[354] The house began to fall into disrepair after the 1960's due to declining membership and changing demographics.[355] In 1986, the building was heavily damaged by a large Magnolia tree which fell against the building. The building was repaired but suffered heavy damage again in 1994 during Hurricane Opal.[356] Currently the building is owned by a developer. The property is vacant, boarded up and for sale as of the date of this writing.

The historic DAR Chapter House, located on Piedmont Avenue just south of 14th, sits in a state of decay and disrepair. It is on the Atlanta Preservation Center's most endangered list. The building is one of Atlanta's last ties to the 1895 Cotton States and International Exposition.

Peachtree by Another Name Would Have Been Grand:

In 1894, certain residents of Pryor Street put forth the idea of changing their street's name.[357] At the time, Pryor ran in almost a straight line "from Clark University to the Grand Opera House and then northerly as Peachtree."[358] The proponents of the name change suggested "that residents of Peachtree Street might want to join in the creation of one long cross-town drive to be known as "Grand Avenue."[359] Garrett writes that "[t]he people of Peachtree, however, with great love and sentiment for their ancient and historic street designation, took a dim view of the proposal," as did the city council.[360] Accordingly "Peachtree" was not lost. One would hope that today's city council would take a similar view of such a proposal.

The 1895 Cotton States and International Exposition:

The 1895 Cotton States and International Exposition occurred at Piedmont Park, then known as the Piedmont Exposition Grounds, and lasted 100 days. It was comprised of 6,000 exhibits and pulled in 800,000 visitors.[361] The name "Cotton States and International" arose in part from a desire to stimulate trade with Central and South America.[362] The city council wanted the exposition to be held at Piedmont Park, but the mayor at the time wanted it to be held at Lakewood.[363]

Before planning the buildings, the organizers sought to obtain an appropriation from the federal government. A bill was introduced and a subcommittee hearing was set for mid-May, 1894.[364] L. F. Livingston, Congressman from the Atlanta district, attended the hearing and spoke in favor of the appropriation.[365] The committee chairman asked why the whole nation should spend its money to benefit the 10 or 12 states that grew cotton.³⁶⁶ Livingston replied cleverly that it was "for the benefit of all those who grow cotton and all those who *wear* cotton."³⁶⁷ (Emphasis added). As a result, Congress appropriated $200,000 for a government exhibit at the Exposition.³⁶⁸

Atlanta gained at least two prominent residents as a result of the Cotton States Exposition. Garrett writes that Ivan Allen, from Dalton, Georgia, founder of the Ivan Allen Company and progenitor of a future mayor of Atlanta, as well as Harry G. Hastings, from Interlachen, Florida, founder of Hastings Seed Company, both visited the Exposition and were inspired to move to Atlanta.³⁶⁹

When Football Was Banned in Atlanta:

On October 30, 1897, University of Georgia fullback Richard "Von" Gammon of Rome, Georgia suffered a concussion during the second half of the game against the University of Virginia.³⁷⁰ Virginia won 17-4. Tragically, he died the next day.³⁷¹ Garrett writes that "[p]ractically every southern college immediately discontinued its football schedule."³⁷²

Garrett further explains that trustees of most of the institutions were summoned for the purpose of discontinuing their football programs permanently, and Atlanta's city council outlawed the game within the city limits.³⁷³ Football in the South was saved, however, because Mrs. Gammon, the mother of Richard Gammon, wrote a letter to the board of trustees of the University of Georgia stating that it was her son's dying wish that the football program should be continued and encouraged.³⁷⁴ As a result of the letter, the trustees threw their full support behind the University of Georgia football program.³⁷⁵ The Atlanta ordinance was repealed prior to the start of the 1898 football season, most likely due to constituents' outcry or a very real concern that hell might otherwise freeze over.

Woodruff at Woodward:

Georgia Military Academy was founded in College Park in 1900 by Colonel John Charles Woodward. The school was organized as a result of a movement by College Park citizens who wanted a military academy in their community.[376] Among other famous alumni, Robert Woodruff, longtime president and chairman of the Coca-Cola Company and beloved Atlanta philanthropist, was sent to Georgia Military Academy after flunking out of Boys High School.[377] The academy was known, at that time, for the importance it placed on discipline, sometimes over academics. The name was changed to Woodward Academy in 1966 in honor of the school's founder.[378]

What Steel Hoops For Cotton Bales Has To Do With Atlantic Station:

Prior to 1901, there were no manufacturers of steel hoops to bind cotton bales, even though the southern states were the largest consumer of these items.[379] A certain George Washington Conners, a 37 year-old junior partner at a mortgage loan and real estate firm, is credited with assembling a group of investors to establish a steel hoop mill in Atlanta.[380] In March, 1901, the Atlanta Steel Hoop Company was incorporated and property for the plant was acquired shortly thereafter.[381] Part of the Civil War Battle of Peachtree Creek had been fought on the property that was selected.[382] In early 1907, the name of the company was changed to "Atlanta Steel Company."[383] Thomas K. Glenn became president of the company on February 1, 1908.[384] Glenn had been vice president of the Georgia Railway & Electric Company, predecessor to the Georgia Power Company prior to that time.[385] The name was again changed to "Atlantic Steel Company." The steam whistle, which blew at 7:00 a.m. every morning, and could be heard from at least 10 miles away, was called "Big Tom" as a memorial to Tom Glenn.[386] The site of the Atlantic Steel Company was subsequently repurposed and redeveloped, and is now the site of Atlantic Station.

Bishop Brown's College:

Morris Brown College was organized by the African Methodist Episcopal Church of Georgia.[387] For this purpose, the organization purchased a site at the northeast corner of Boulevard and Houston Street in downtown Atlanta in 1881 for $3,500.00.[388] The first building was erected in 1884.[389] Originally, only high school classes were offered. In 1894, however, the trustees organized a liberal arts college and established a department of theology.[390] In 1932, a prep school was established and in the same year the school moved to its present site.[391] The college was named for Morris Brown, a bishop in the African Methodist Episcopal Church.[392]

Atlanta Gets the Bird and other Cliff Clavin-worthy Triva:

In 1916, the Georgia Legislature passed a bill authorizing women to practice law in Georgia courts, even though women were not yet allowed to vote.[393] It also adopted the Cherokee Rose as the official flower of the state the same year.[394]

The present official seal of Atlanta was adopted in 1887.[395] The Phoenix pictured on the seal is rising from the flames of its destruction. The dates (1847-1865) represent the incorporation and rebuilding of Atlanta. The Latin "resurgens" means rising again.

There were 1,400 Germans soldiers interned at Ft. McPherson in 1918.[396]

In 1919, there was a movement initiated to make Macon, Georgia, the state capital.[397] The Atlanta Chamber of Commerce successfully quashed the proposed action shortly thereafter.[398]

Legendary dancing instructor Arthur Murray lived at the Georgian Terrace Hotel and attended Georgia Tech in 1919.[399] Garrett writes that "it was in Atlanta that the inspiration came to him to teach his dancing methods by correspondence, a procedure which started him toward his million dollar goal."[400]

Hotel Fires Prior to and Including the Winecoff:

There were three major hotel fires in Atlanta prior to the Winecoff tragedy. They were: the Kimball House fire of 1883, the Markham House fire in 1896, and the Wilson Hotel fire of November 7, 1919.[401] Fortunately, no one died in the first two of these fires.[402] But four of the twenty-five guests in the Wilson Hotel at the time of that fire did not survive.[403]

America's worst hotel fire occurred on December 7, 1946, when 119 people lost their lives in the Winecoff Hotel Fire. The majority of the victims were young boys and girls in town for a YMCA meeting.[404] The builder, W. F. Winecoff and his wife, who were permanent residents of the building, also died in the fire. The Winecoff was not completely destroyed, however, and the rebuilt building stands today at 176 Peachtree Street as the Ellis Hotel.

The Ellis Hotel in downtown Atlanta was, at one time, the Winecoff Hotel, which is where, on December 7, 1946, the worst hotel fire in U.S. history occurred.

Famous Landmarks:

The Castle, was originally known as "Fort Place." Ferdinand McMillan, a dealer in agricultural machinery built the home in 1910. At the time, the front yard was "a veritable farm in the midst of the city."[405]

Located on 15th Street in Midtown, across from the Woodruff Arts Center, the Castle with its fortress-like walls which include embrasures, still stands and is currently being repurposed.

De Give's original opera house later became the Columbia Theater and then the Bijou "in its declining years."[406] It was located at the corner of Marietta and Forsyth streets for 50 years.[407] In 1921, it was torn down and the Palmer Building was constructed on the site.[408]

You Can Bank on It:

The Atlanta State Savings Bank was the first African-American-owned bank in Atlanta. The bank was organized in 1909 by John O. Ross, who owned grocery stores on West Hunter and Butler streets.[409] Garrett writes that the bank failed in 1922, but that it paved the way for the Citizens Trust Company.[410] Citizens Trust Company opened on August 16, 1921, in Atlanta as a result of the vision of Herman E. Perry, James A. Robinson, Thomas J. Ferguson, W. H. King and H. C. Dugas, five African-American men known as the "Fervent Five."[411] Perry had founded Standard Life Insurance Company in 1909, which by 1921 had become the largest African-American-owned insurance company in the U.S.[412] The bank's mission was to serve the credit and deposit needs of African-American citizens of Atlanta. Citizens Trust Bank's current headquarters at 75 Piedmont Avenue was built in 1969.[413]

The Fourth National Bank was the first national bank to employ a female teller and to establish a savings department.[414] It was originally a state-chartered bank known as the American Trust and Banking Company.[415] The president was Captain James W. English and the bank was often called "Captain English's Bank."[416] In 1896, the bank was converted into a national bank and became the Fourth National Bank.[417] The Fourth National Bank moved to the corner of Peachtree and Marietta Streets and merged with the

Atlanta and Lowry National Bank to form First National Bank in 1919 (now Wells Fargo Bank).[418]

Neighborhood Naissance:

On May 18, 1908, Asa G. Candler, Preston S. Arkwright and George Adair purchased 1,492 acres on the northeastern edge of Atlanta for $500,000.[419] The land was subsequently developed as Druid Hills and was, at that time, the largest real estate transaction in the Southeast.[420]

The neighborhood to the east of Piedmont Park where Orme Circle is located was originally called Boulevard Park. The owner of the 64.5 acres now comprising the neighborhood, Dr. Henry L. Wilson, sold it to the North Boulevard Park Corporation on August 20, 1914. Lots were developed and originally sold for $10,000 per acre.[421] The land had been dormant for some time as it was cut off by the valley of Clear Creek.[422] A bridge built over the creek and the Southern Railway rail line connected the land to Piedmont Park and made it more attractive to developers. Orme Circle was named after Atlanta Electric Light Company Official Aquilla J. Orme. Orme had approved a plan to extend the trolley line from downtown Atlanta to the Old Soldier's Home on East Confederate Avenue.[423] Ormewood Park, which sprang up because of this new line, also bears his name.[424]

The Kirkwood neighborhood was originally its own city (incorporated in 1899) before it was annexed into the City of Atlanta. In 1922, it became the twelfth Ward of the City of Atlanta.[425]

In 1923, development began on Morningside Park by James R. Smith and M. S. Rankin.[426] B. F. and A. C. Burdett began developing Brookwood Hills out of the old Andrew Jackson Collier estate the same year.[427]

Berkeley Park, the neighborhood between Howell Mill and Northside Drive just west of I-75, was developed in 1924 by the E. Rivers Realty Company.[428]

Phillips C. McDuffie developed Garden Hills in 1925.[429]

During 1926 and 1927, Eugene V. Haynes, a well-known jeweler turned real estate developer, developed Haynes Manor.[430] Garrett writes that the presence of the sewage disposal plant south of Peachtree Creek and just east of Northside Drive was "a definite detriment to the project."[431] It was moved during the 1930's when the Clayton Plant on South Atlanta Road was built.[432]

Ansley Park, originally called Peachtree Garden, was carved out of the George W. Collier estate in 1904.[433]

Early Churches:

Although it did not have a permanent building, North Avenue Presbyterian Church was organized on December 4, 1889.[434] $19,000 was raised for the construction of the church, and $18,000 was spent for the lot where the church now stands.[435] The granite for the building was quarried from Stone Mountain and donated by the Venable family. The new church was first occupied on Thanksgiving Day, 1900.[436]

The first home to be built in Druid Hills was built by Judge John S. Candler, Asa Candler's older brother. It was built in 1909, on the northeast corner of Ponce de Leon Avenue and Briarcliff Road. The house was built on 4.5 acres and was unique at the time because it had four bathrooms, one for each bedroom.[437] It was torn down in 1952, and the Druid Hills Methodist Church now stands on the site.

Located across from the Plaza Theater on Ponce, the Druid Hills Methodist Church stands on the former site of Judge John S. Candler's home. John Candler, Asa's older brother, had introduced Asa to the start-up which Asa bought and developed into the Coca-Cola Company.

Multiple Mansions:

The original governor's mansion was located at 1798 Peachtree Road, which was owned by W. W. Brookes and leased to the state.[438] The governor's residence was moved in October, 1924 to 205 The Prado in Ansley Park. This residence was also originally leased by the State before it purchased the property.[439] The home was made of granite, some of which was actually quarried from the hill on which the house is located.[440] The house was built by Edwin P. Ansley (the developer of Ansley Park). The present governor's mansion, which is located on West Paces Ferry Road, was constructed in 1967.

The House That Jack Built:

Prior to its demolition, the Richardson building was located at 160 Peachtree Street and known as "The House That Jack Built."[441] It was built by Jasper Newton "Jack" Smith in 1889. Adorning the front entrance were two stone blocks, both of which contained interesting inscriptions. One block read "This is the House That Jack Built."[442] The other stone read "J. J. Smith's Building: Commenced 100 years after George Washington's inauguration as President - Paul says: Owe No Man: - Let Posterity Heed His Advice."[443] In 1909, Smith leased the building and the land to Edward W. Alfriend for $2,000 per year for 99 years.[444] It was one of the first long-term leases made in Atlanta, and "was considered at the time to be a mad undertaking for Mr. Alfriend."[445] Not that mad however; Alfriend sold the lease to Hugh Richardson 15 years later for $150,000.[446]

In the lease to Alfriend, Smith required that the two stone blocks remain there, and if the building were torn down, they must be incorporated into the new building built there.[447] Accordingly, when Richardson rebuilt the building, he had the blocks inserted above the cornice.[448] A small MARTA building currently occupies the site but there is no evidence of the two stone blocks. As the requirement for incorporating the stone blocks was in a lease which expired in 1989, rather than a covenant which ran with the land, MARTA was likely not subject to the requirement.

Historic Hotels: More Than You Can Bare

The Clermont Hotel was built in 1924, and was originally known as the Bonaventure Arms.[449] In the hotel's declining years, the establishment located in the basement known as the Clermont Lounge has offered more Atlantans than will admit it quite a bon adventure as well.

"The Biltmore, the Robert Fulton (later the Georgian) and the Henry Grady were all completed and opened between April and November, 1924."[450] The total construction bill for The Biltmore ran approximately $6,000,000.[451]

Built in 1924, The Robert Fulton was, at 15 stories, Atlanta's tallest hotel at the time.[452] It was designed by E. C. Saiz and built by Ben J. Massell.[453] The Robert Fulton was located at the corner of Cone and Lucky streets downtown. The hotel was sold to Fred B. Wilson for $850,000 in 1950, and shortly thereafter, the name was changed to the Georgian.[454] Unfortunately, the hotel was demolished in 1971 and replaced with a parking garage.

Development of Avondale Estates Funded by Drug Money:

George Frances Willis was born in Waynesville, North Carolina around 1880.[455] After attending a military academy in Ashville, North Carolina, he moved to Knoxville, Tennessee, where he took a job with a company making proprietary medicines.[456] Willis founded International Proprietaries, Inc. in 1913. Garrett notes that Willis was a salesman, not a chemist and in 1922, he sold the company for $1,000,000.[457] Willis made a fortune off Tanlac and another chemical called Zonite, an antiseptic used in World War I.[458] In 1924, Willis purchased the town of Ingleside, Georgia, and 950 acres of adjoining land, "which he intended to develop into a model residential suburb."[459] For four years, with funds from Tanlac and Zonite sales, Willis developed farm land into Avondale Estates. Garrett writes that Willis's money ran out, but Willis was working on a chemical called Sargon and was "well on his way to a third fortune when he died in July, 1932."[460] Avondale Estates became the City of Avondale Estates by legislative action approved August 25, 1926.[461] The population was 750 in 1928.[462]

If It Could Grow as Hard as It Could Blow:

By the summer of 1925, the Florida real estate boom had taken off.[463] Garrett cites an article by Hal Stead which reads:

> **Property in Miami changed hands so fast that it was never delivered to the buyers. You bought contracts of sale - binders they were called - and you sold your binder to the next eager buyer, and he to the next, and so on. The title companies were swamped. The real estate agencies kept open house, with band concerts and teas, and stayed open all night.**[464]

The Florida boom was the catalyst for the first Forward Atlanta campaign. Atlanta faced an economic slump due to an exodus of labor, capital and customers to Florida.[465] A group of business leaders got together in October, 1925, and came up with the idea of organizing a nationwide campaign to promote Atlanta, dubbed "Forward Atlanta."[466] The Forward Atlanta Commission, chaired by Ivan Allen was composed of:

Frank Adair	Chark Howell, Jr.	J. K. Orr
Ivan Allen	Harry H. Johnson	J. K. Ottley
Philip H. Alston	Dr. Herbert Kennedy	Emmett Quinn
Charles D. Atkinson	Roy Le Craw	Ronald Ransom
Benjamin S. Barker	N. Baxter Maddox	W. R. C. Smith
L. H. Beall	George Marchmont	James L. Wells
Milton Bell	Louis P. Marquardt	George W. West

William Candler	Virlyn B. Moore	Russell Whitman
Milton Dargan, Jr.	Wiley L. Moore	J. H. Woody
Jackson P. Dick	L. T. Y. Nash	H. Lane Young[467]
Henderson Hallman	Frank Neely	
George M. Hope	A.J. Orme	

The commission created a nationwide advertising campaign which promoted the Atlanta region's climate, labor supply, location and abundant natural resources.

Can You Envision It?

Up until 1925, the bridge over the Chattahoochee River where Roswell Road crosses the river was a weather-beaten wooden covered bridge. It was replaced with a concrete bridge which was dedicated on July 17, 1925.[468] The site of the covered bridge is currently marked with an interpretative sign along the City of Roswell Riverwalk Trail.

Clearly This Must Have Gone Off Without a Hitch:

Atlanta's first street numbers were set in 1873, but the numbering had become "unintelligible" by 1891, so the streets were renumbered.[469] By 1926, due to the growth of the city, a second renumbering became necessary. It was at this time that the city was divided into four sections (N.E., N.W., S.E. and S.W.). The intersection of the lines dividing the four sections was at the corner of Pryor Street and Edgewood Avenue, the corner of Land Lots 51, 52, 77 and 78.[470] The base lines of the quadrants then followed the land lot lines. Street numbers were then assigned every 20 feet with the numbers growing higher the farther the distance from the base line intersection.[471] However, because "the streets in Ansley Park simply could not be made to conform to the base lines," its original house numbers remain.[472]

The History of Atlanta History:

There were two failed attempts at an Atlanta historical organization, the Atlanta Pioneer and Historic Society in the 1870's and the Pioneer Citizens' Society in the 1890's.[473] In 1926, however, real traction was made in forming a permanent Atlanta historical organization. Inspired by Walter McElreath, an attorney and former Fulton County representative in the state legislature, a group of Atlantans obtained a charter for The Atlanta Historical Society.[474]

The Atlanta Historical Society originally planned to construct a building on a lot it purchased in 1940 at the southwest corner of Peachtree and Sixteenth streets.[475] Due to skyrocketing construction costs during World War II, however, the society scrapped those plans and decided to purchase an existing building instead.

In late 1846, the home of Dr. and Mrs. Willis B. Jones at the southeast corner of Peachtree and Huntington roads was purchased and the house was named McElreath Hall.[476]

The current campus of the Atlanta Historical Society on West Paces Ferry Road was acquired in 1966.[477] It is the former estate of the Edward and Emily Inman family. Their grand mansion, the iconic Swan House, built in 1928 and designed by Philip Trammell Shutze, forms an integral part of the campus.

The Swan House, built in 1928, and located on the Atlanta History Center Campus, is open to the public. Its original owner, Edward Inman, raced cars as a hobby at The Atlanta Speedway, later Candler Field (still later site of Hartsfield-Jackson International Airport). His trophies are still in the house.

Before the iPhone:

Atlanta was the first city in the South to receive the service known as telephotophy, where pictures were transmitted by wire.[478] On January 9, 1927, the debut was made at the Telephone Building at the northeast corner of Pryor and Mitchell streets.[479] According to Garrett, "among the features of the January 9 demonstration was an exchange of pictured greetings between Bobby Jones and George Van Elan, another noted golfer, in Los Angeles."[480]

Landing an Airport:

In the summer of 1909, at the urging of his eccentric son Asa, Jr., Asa G. Candler purchased 300 acres of land near Hapeville, Georgia, which later became the nucleus for Hartsfield-Jackson International Airport.[481] Candler organized a company called the Atlanta Automobile Association and built the Atlanta Speedway on the property.[482] The property was also known as Candler Field.

Candler Field was purchased by the City of Atlanta for a municipal airport in 1929.[483] The purchase price was $94,500 and the closing occurred on April 13, 1929.[484] The passenger terminal was situated to utilize large existing runways donated by the Army. The terminal was built mostly out of war surplus materials and cost approximately $270,000.[485]

Because Parents Didn't Have Xanax Back Then:

The Fritz Orr Club - Camp School was organized in the fall of 1929.[486] The idea was the brainchild of prominent Atlanta attorney Charles B. Shelton and his wife who had four young sons.[487] The Sheltons' idea was to start a camp program for boys during the winter months-- the very months when four boys cooped up indoors would tend to drive their parents to distraction. The Sheltons tapped Fritz Orr to run the camp. He was a 24-year-old math instructor at the University School for Boys.[488] Orr was also a UGA grad, native of Athens, a cross-country runner and was active with the YMCA.[489] The camp was started with 12 boys and camp activities were held at the Shelton estate. In just three years, it grew to 100 boys and a permanent site was acquired at the intersection of Nancy Creek and West Paces Ferry roads.[490] The camp and camp property was subsequently acquired by The Westminster Schools and is used during the school year primarily for the school's lacrosse program.

Too Big to Flail:

On November 25, 1929, with over $140,000,000.00 of combined resources, the First National Bank of Atlanta was formed out of a merger of Atlanta's two largest banks, the Atlanta and Lowery National Bank and the Fourth National Bank.[491] It was the 15th largest bank in the country at the time and came together very quickly. Robert Woodruff, president of the Coca-Cola Company, had initiated the idea just three months prior.[492] The officers of the new bank were John K. Ottley, president (formerly president of the Fourth National Bank) Thomas K. Glenn, chairman (former president of the Atlanta and Lowry Banks) and James D. Robinson, Sr., executive vice president.[493]

How Roswell Got Stuck With Fulton County Taxes:

In 1931, a state program called "Bigger and Better Counties" led to the merger of Milton and Campbell counties into Fulton.[494] Georgia has relatively small counties due to the fact that when the counties were created and the lines were drawn, the intent was to leave no citizen more than a day's wagon ride to the county seat. A problem arose with this merger because the most direct route from existing Fulton County to the newly added Fulton County territory was through the Roswell district of Cobb County. Problem solved: in May of 1932, the Roswell Militia District, which included the town of Roswell, was transferred to Fulton County.[495]

Lenox Square (Formerly Joyeuse Estate) Scene of First Executive Kidnapping:

John K. Ottley, president of First National Bank, was kidnapped on the morning of July 6, 1933. As Ottley exited his driveway at his estate at 3415 Peachtree Road at about 8:00 a.m., he pulled over to give a hitchhiker a ride to town.[496] Ottley was familiar with the man because he had been operating a fruit stand in the vicinity for a period of time.[497] The man stuck a pistol in Ottley's side and ordered him into the back seat.[498] The kidnapper's accomplice, Pryor Bowen, 17, jumped in the car and took the wheel. The two drove Ottley out Peachtree Road to Suwanee, Georgia.[499]

The older kidnapper, addressed as "Grover" ordered Bowen to turn off onto a dirt road which led to the Chattahoochee River.[500] Bowen stayed with Ottley while Grover went back to Atlanta to deliver a ransom note for $40,000.00. Ottley had noticed that Bowen was not fully committed to the kidnapping. After Grover left, Ottley persuaded Bowen to untie him and remove his blindfold.[501] Ottley and Bowen began to walk back to Suwanee and they soon ran into two locals who obtained a small truck and all four drove into Suwanee.[502] Ottley called his home and the bank to report that he was safe. Grover delivered a ransom note addressed to Mrs. Ottley at their home, "Joyeuse" on Peachtree Road, but Mrs. Ottley was at Tallulah Falls, Georgia, at the time.[503] The ransom note was delivered to the caretaker at Joyeuse and read as follows:

> **Your husband has been kidnapped. We are holding him for $40,000. If you notify the authorities, the police, the newspapers or anyone else, he will be killed. Instructions later. Get the money immediately--today if possible. Do you want your money or your husband? The money in $5, $10, $20, $50 bills. Which shall it be? If anyone asks about him say he was called out of the city for a few days. When I contact with you I will be known as E.M.**[504]

The news that Ottley was safe hit the news wires immediately and Grover disappeared without attempting to collect the ransom. A manhunt was immediately initiated to track him down. Bowen was taken into custody in

Suwanee, and although Ottley did not press charges, Bowen was sentenced to one year on the chain gang.[505] "Grover", whose real name was William Randolph Dilensky, was captured on August 5, 1933, in San Antonio, Texas.[506] He was returned to Atlanta, where he confessed and was sentenced to 21 to 28 years. Dilensky was paroled however in 1949.[507] According to Garrett, "Mr. Ottley was shaken, but not permanently injured as a result of the experience. All he lost was the ten-dollar bill he had on his person at the time and his glasses."[508] He was home in time for dinner. A first-hand account by Ottley's son of the kidnapping and the apprehension of Dilensky is reprinted in Appendix 1.

The Back Story on Gone With The Wind:

The publishing and media phenomenon that is *Gone With The Wind* came about in part because a certain H. S. Latham, vice president of the McMillan Company, visited Georgia in 1935 "in search of a southern novel."[509]

Margaret Mitchell, who had been a reporter for the *Atlanta Journal* from 1922 to 1926, helped round up other Atlanta authors for Latham's consideration during his visit.[510] It was at a tea given in Latham's honor that he learned that Mitchell was an author herself and had written a southern novel.[511] Upon Latham's request, Mitchell provided him with 60 large manila envelopes containing the manuscript.[512] Margaret Mitchell worked on the book approximately 10 years and never thought of having it published according to an article by Yolande Gwin published in The *Atlanta Constitution*.[513] Incredibly, Mitchell then changed her mind about submitting the manuscript for consideration and wired Latham in Charlotte, New Orleans and San Francisco to send it back. Latham either did not receive the wires or chose to ignore them. In San Francisco, Latham advised Mitchell that her book had been accepted.[514] Mitchell was quoted as saying "[i]t was then that I went to bed. The shock was too great. If I had had any idea that my book was salable, I would have stormed the markets long ago."[515]

Mitchell started *GWTW* in 1925, "merely as a method of amusement," the rationale being that "the jazz age was at its height…[and] a book dealing with these customs and conventions would hardly have been appreciated."[516] In 1929, Mitchell had written all but three chapters and gave it up, mainly because she had never intended to try to have it published.[517] Mitchell stated that the manuscript "was a big help around the house for such necessary notations as party and grocery lists, various recipes and telephone numbers."[518] It apparently contained multiple coffee stains as well since Mitchell wrote "during her late breakfast hour."[519] Interestingly enough, Mitchell stated she "loathe[d] writing and…made no plans for [her] future work."[520]

Mitchell did not expect the book to even sell 5,000 copies, and the McMillan Company only printed 10,000 copies for the first edition, but the book surpassed that sales target even before its official publication date.[521] As of 2012, *Gone With the Wind* has sold more than 30 million copies worldwide.[522]

Famous Roads:

On June 30, 1937, the development of Georgia's first four lane highway, U.S. Highway 41, was announced.[523] The first link of the "Atlanta-Marietta highway [which] extended from a point on Northside Drive near

Arden Road to the old Marietta Highway #41 at a point north of Marietta was opened in May, 1938."[524]

Cheshire Bridge Road was named after Napolean H. Cheshire who was a member of the 22nd Georgia Regiment of Confederate Cavalry and a son of early settler Hezekiah Cheshire.[525] Napolean H. Cheshire died in 1921.[526]

In 1927, Mayson Avenue, named after the Mayson family who lived in the area, was renamed Lindbergh Drive in honor of Colonel Charles A. Lindbergh, the first aviator to fly from New York to Paris.[527]

Gone With The Wind Factoids:

Friday, December 15, 1939, was the premiere of the movie of "Gone With The Wind."[528] David O. Selznick had purchased the movie rights on July 30, 1936, for $50,000.00. At the time, it was the highest price ever paid for a first novel.[529] The recreated City of Atlanta set was the largest movie set ever built, consisting of 53 buildings and 7,000 feet of streets.[530]

The "Gone With The Wind" title is a quotation from the late 19th century English poem *"Non Sum Qualis eram Bonae Sub Regno Cynarae."* One verse reads: "I have forgot much, Cynara! Gone with the wind, Flung roses, roses riotously with the throng, Dancing to put thy pale, lost lilies out of mind."[531] *Non Sum Qualis eram Bonae Sub Regno Cynarae* translates "I am not what I was under the reign of the good Cynara", which is a quotation from Horace's Odes, Book IV, I.[532] According to Margaret Mitchell, it was the "far away, faintly sad sound I wanted."[533]

The author of the poem, Earnest Dowson, fell in love at the age of 23 with an 11-year-old Adelaide "Missy" Foltinowicz and it is Missy who is purportedly the subject of *Cynarae*.[534] His love was unrequited and, in 1897, she married a tailor who lived above her father's restaurant.[535] Dowson was crushed and died of alcoholism in 1900 at the age of 32.[536] Oddly enough, Dowson's other claim to fame was being credited as the first person to use the word "soccer" in written language, although he spelled it "socca."[537]

Upon her arrival in Atlanta for the world premiere of the movie, Vivian Leigh was chauffeured from the airport with producer David O. Selznick and Mayor Hartsfield to the Georgian Terrace Hotel behind a motorcycle police escort.[538] Her first words were purportedly "Look! There's that red dirt we've been working in."[539]

In Search of Scarlett:

A national search was conducted for the woman to play Scarlett O'Hara.[540] According to Garrett, "1,400 candidates were interviewed, 90 were screen tested, 149,000 feet of black and white film and 13,000 feet of Technicolor was shot in those tests."[541] The cost of the search was computed at "$92,000." Whereas, the casting of the other 59 characters cost only $10,000.[542] Interestingly enough, filming began before Scarlett had been cast.[543]

The scene depicting the burning of the military supplies of Atlanta was filmed on the night of December 14, 1938.[544] It was during the filming of this scene that Selznick met Vivian Leigh. She was a spectator who had accompanied Selznick's brother Myron, a well-known agent, to the studio.[545]

Selznick screen tested Vivian Leigh on January 16, 1939 and signed her for the role.[546]

Famous Guests of Atlanta's Alcatraz:

By an act of the Legislature, in December of 1899, the State of Georgia ceded to the U.S. Government jurisdiction to the 300-acre tract selected for a federal penitentiary.[547] The Atlanta Penitentiary opened its doors in January, 1902, and Garrett writes that the great prison wall, enclosing 28 acres, though not visible from space, was "the largest reinforced steel and concrete structure in the world."[548] It was "4,178 feet long, between 28 and 37 feet high, and from 2 to 4 feet thick."[549] "Dutch" Anderson and Gerald Chapman (who became famous by virtue of their attempted escape) tunneled under the prison wall, however, and Chapman, though not his partner, actually did get away.[550] According to Garrett, Al Capone spent time in the Atlanta Federal Penitentiary as did Nathaniel Hawthorne's son Julian Hawthorne, who was convicted of mail fraud in 1913.[551]

Hermi's Bridge:

The old iron bridge spanning the Chattahoochee over Paces Ferry Road was built in 1904.[552] It was built just south of the actual ferry crossing of Hardy Pace.[553] It was financed jointly by Cobb and Fulton counties and cost approximately $10,000.[554] The first citizen to cross the bridge was Judge Charles A. Howell, a brother of then Atlanta Mayor Evan P. Howell.[555] Judge E. B. Rosser, chairman of the Fulton County Roads and Bridges Committee, led the effort to build the bridge and convinced Cobb County to share the cost of the bridge.[556] An article in the *Atlanta Journal* about the opening of the bridge indicated that there was a strong sentiment among residents to name the bridge after Rosser, which apparently did not occur.[557]

Fulton County planned to tear down the bridge and replace it with a new one in 1972. At that time, prominent Atlanta architect Cecil Alexander and his wife Hermione ("Hermi") set out to save the bridge.[558] Cecil had grown up in the area and had spent "lazy summer days walking beneath the bridge as a child."[559] Cecil and Hermi succeeded in saving the bridge, convincing the Fulton County Commission that it would be more cost effective to leave the old bridge in place and build the new bridge beside it.[560] Eleven years later, on the night of October 25, 1983, Cecil and Hermi were hit by a 16-year-old drunk driver.[561] Hermi was killed and Cecil suffered a broken hip and other injuries.[562] Michael Lomax, then Fulton County Commissioner, visited Cecil in the hospital and asked if there was anything he could do for him.[563] Cecil asked if the county could rename the bridge for Hermi, and Lomax wholeheartedly agreed.[564] In 1984, a resolution was passed by Fulton County officially naming the bridge for Hermi.[565] Hermi's Bridge is now a pedestrian bridge connecting runners, walkers and bikers from Buckhead to Vinings.

Spanning the Chattahoochee near the site of the former Hardy Pace Ferry, the (now) baby blue steel bridge, was built in 1904. It was saved from destruction by "Hermi" and Cecil Alexander. The pedestrian bridge now bears Hermi's name; Hermi was killed by a drunk driver in 1983.

The Low-Down on the High:

The High Museum of Art was founded as the Atlanta Art Association and was chartered on June 28, 1895.[566] In 1924, the City of Atlanta Park Commission voted to give the association a "ten acre site in Piedmont Park for a city-owned museum, but the property was never used."[567] Garrett quips that "[h]igh tide for the Art Association came in 1926," when Mrs. Joseph Madison High, donated her home just north of 15th Street on Peachtree to the association for a museum.[568] The museum opened in October, 1926.[569] The first picture acquired by the museum was F. Luis Mora's *Spanish Souvenir*, which was purchased in 1930.[570]

Pre-Piedmont and Early Emory:

The hospitals which became Emory University Hospital and Piedmont Hospital each began operating on a small scale in 1905.[571] The original name of the former was Wesley Memorial Hospital and was organized by Asa G. Candler and his younger brother, Warren. Candler bought and donated a house at the corner of Courtland Street and Auburn Avenue known as the "Calico House," and the hospital opened in it August 16, 1905 with 50 beds.[572] Through the efforts of Candler and others, a new hospital on the Emory University Campus was opened October 5, 1920. The 26 patients at the Calico House were transported to the new hospital in vehicles "lent by the morticians of Atlanta."[573] For those patients still under the fog of anesthesia, departing the hospital in a hearse must have been somewhat disconcerting. In approximately 1925, the name was changed to Emory University Hospital.[574]

Piedmont Hospital, originally Piedmont Sanatorium, was the successor to Amster's Private Sanitorium.[575] That facility was founded by Dr.

Ludwig Amster and was located at the northwest corner of Capitol Avenue and Cromley Street.[576] The hospital purchased the land for its present campus on Peachtree Road in 1943 and broke ground for the new hospital in 1954.[577] The new (present) location was previously the estate of Jack J. Spalding, the founder of King and Spalding law firm, and known as "Deerland."[578]

The Candler Building, Worth a Closer Look:

Asa G. Candler's first large real estate enterprise was the design and construction of the Candler Building. Financed by loans from the Coca-Cola Company, the building was completed in December, 1906.[579]

Sculptures of Candler's parents set in Georgia marble adorn the lobby as a tribute.[580] Ornamental friezes of Sidney Lanier, after whom Lake Lanier was named, Joel Chandler Harris, editor of The *Atlanta Constitution*, and Eli Whitney, inventor of the cotton gin, also are in the building. Between the first and second stories, there are carved panels of Michelangelo, Raphael, Shakespeare and Wagner.[581]

Candler wanted a bank to occupy the ground floor believing it would increase the building's prestige, so Candler organized his own bank to locate there.[582] Candler's bank, The Central Bank & Trust Corporation, opened in February 6, 1906, and later merged with C&S Bank, which became Nationsbank, then later Bank of America.[583]

Built in 1906, the Candler building, located on the corner of Peachtree Street and John Wesley Dobbs Avenue in downtown Atlanta, was Asa Candler's first large real estate project, and was financed with loans from the Coca-Cola Company.

Sculptures and friezes grace both the interior and exterior of the Candler building. Carvings of Shakespeare and Michelangelo and Raphael, among others, adorn panels between the first and second floors.

Piedmont Driving Club Almost *Ansley Park* Driving Club:

On January 11, 1906, a fire broke out in Piedmont Park which destroyed two of the 1895 Exposition buildings and badly damaged the Piedmont Driving Club clubhouse.[584] The building was so damaged that "the members of the Driving Club gave serious consideration to rebuilding farther out."[585] Edwin P. Ansley offered to trade 50 acres in Ansley Park for the five acres that the club owned.[586] Garrett writes that the offer was seriously considered, and voted on, but ultimately declined.[587] As mentioned previously, a portion of the clubhouse building dates back to the Reconstruction Era. Prior to 1887, the land where Piedmont Park sits today, along with the Piedmont Driving Club property was the farm of Benjamin F. "Doc" Walker, son of the pioneer Samuel Walker.[588] Samuel Walker originally purchased the property in 1834 for $450 when it was still part of DeKalb County.[589] Benjamin bought the property from his father on January 2, 1857. In 1868, he built a stone residence which formed the nucleus of the clubhouse building of the Piedmont Driving Club city club.[590]

The Grove Park Inn - William Randolph Hearst - Atlanta Connection:

On April 25, 1906, a certain Fred Loring Seely, who was originally from Orange, New Jersey, founded the newspaper, *The Atlanta Georgian*.[591] Garrett describes the paper as "[o]ne of the most colorful newspapers in the history of Atlanta journalism."[592] Seely sold out to William Randolph Hearst in 1912. After the sale, Seely moved to Ashville, North Carolina, where he built the Grove Park Inn.[593]

Why We Won't See a Streetcar in the Median of Ponce de Leon Avenue:

Ponce de Leon Avenue used to be configured as two opposite lanes (each 30' wide) separated by a 30-foot strip of land that was privately owned by the Atlanta Street Railway Company.[594] Back in 1871, the company had operated a horse-drawn trolley line which ferried passengers to Ponce de Leon Springs (now the site of the City Hall East building) for its medicinal purposes. In 1907, the Georgia Railway & Electric Company, successor-in-interest to the Atlanta Street Railway Company, dedicated this strip to the city, but with the reservation that no other transit companies be allowed to use the strip.[595]

When Did Peachtree Get So Wide?

The widening of Peachtree Road north of the Brookwood Bridge into an 80 foot-wide boulevard was completed in 1908.[596] Property owners on either side donated 10 feet of their property for the widening project.[597]

Two Places in the Atlanta Area Not Named After a Peach Tree:

A section of Andrew Young International Boulevard was once known as Magnolia Street.[598] Magnolia Street was originally Old Magazine Street, however. Caption W.A. Fuller, famous for chasing the Federals who stole the General in the Great Locomotive Heist during the Civil War, gave Magnolia Street its (new) name in 1885.[599] Captain Fuller lived on Old Magazine Street and prided himself on the beautifully maintained Magnolia trees growing in his front yard, so much so that he had the street renamed "Magnolia Street."[600]

The Oakhurst neighborhood was so named because of the numerous oak trees in the area.[601] Oakhurst was originally incorporated as its own town on April 19, 1909, but was later merged into the City of Decatur.[602]

You Can Pin This One on Flinn:

In 1909, the Rev. Richard Orme Flinn, first pastor of North Avenue Presbyterian Church, and Marion Hull, M.D. began discussing the idea of organizing a school which would have a strong religious emphasis.[603] They proposed the idea to the church members who were receptive.[604] In September, 1909, the school, named the North Avenue Presbyterian School, commenced operations in a Sunday School room at the church on the corner of North Avenue and Peachtree Street. Twenty students were present. The sole teacher was a Miss Emma Askew, an Agnes Scott College graduate.[605] In 1920, the school moved to Ponce de Leon Avenue and in 1951, the name was changed to The Westminster Schools.[606] In approximately 1951, The Westminster Schools moved to its present location on West Paces Ferry Road.

Peachtree Heights Park Formerly Part of Wesley Gray Collier Estate:

Since before the Civil War, and until his death in 1906, the west side of Peachtree Road from Peachtree Creek to the present Andrews Drive was owned by Wesley Gray Collier.[607] It was an approximately 500-acre tract. The executors of his estate, Eretus Rivers and Walter P. Andrews, sold the property to the Peachtree Heights Park Company for $375,000.[608] At that time, Peachtree Battle Avenue had already been cut through to Howell Mill Road, but was known as Battle Avenue.[609] It was likely an easy real estate closing since Mr. Rivers was the seller and buyer. (Rivers developed Peachtree Heights Neighborhood). The takeaway: The "E." in E. Rivers School located in Peachtree Heights neighborhood on the corner of Peachtree Battle Avenue and Peachtree Road stands for "Eretus," not "East."

"Ain't Paying No 50 Cents for No Golf" and Other Atlanta Golf Course Trivia:

The Ansley Park Club golf course began in 1910 as a semi-public golf course with a 15-cent greens fee.[610] It was originally a nine-hole course.[611] In 1913, the greens fee increased to 50 cents. Some of the regular players objected to the fee and, in 1915, decided to form a club in order to keep the greens fees more reasonable.[612]

In 1910, the members of the Mechanical and Manufacturer's Club formed a company and purchased 150 acres on Peachtree Road for the purpose of building the Brookhaven Country Club.[613] The property was formerly owned by Isham Stovall.[614] The golf course opened on Christmas Day, 1911, and was acquired by the Capital City Club in 1913.[615]

The first golf course in Atlanta was built in 1895 on property now encompassed by Piedmont Park, but then owned by the Piedmont Driving Club. It had only seven holes.[616] Garrett writes that this "early experiment was short-lived."[617]

Bobby Jones golf course was built in 1929.[618]

The Wren's Nest:

In 1881, Joel Chandler Harris, famed associate editor of the *Atlanta Constitution*, folklorist, and author of the well-known Uncle Remus stories, moved his family to a 5.25 acre tract in West End.[619] The home is now known as the Wren's Nest. At the time of purchase, it was known as the "Broomhead Property."[620] The original house was much smaller and multiple additions were made to the property over the years. Harris referred to the property as his beloved "Snapbean Farm."[621] Harris died on July 3, 1908, at the age of 59 of uremic poisoning.⁶²² The Wren's Nest is now open to the public for tours and features professional story tellers recounting Harris's famous Brer Rabbit tales. Interestingly enough, Harris's great-grandson is currently the executive director of the Wren's Nest House Museum.

Located in West End, the Wren's Nest was the former home of Joel Chandler Harris, author of the well-known Uncle Remus stories. The Wren's Nest is open to the public and features story tellers recounting those Uncle Remus stories.

Monumental Intersection:

Several monuments have been placed at the intersection of Peachtree and West Peachtree streets. Originally, the Ben Hill Monument was unveiled there in 1886.⁶²³ It was later moved to the state Capitol building to protect it from vandalism. Subsequently, in 1895, the Erskine Memorial Fountain was presented to the city and located at the intersection.⁶²⁴ In 1912, however, the grade of Peachtree and West Peachtree was lowered such that the fountain was "stranded above street level."⁶²⁵ Later that year, the fountain was moved to the Cherokee Avenue-Ormond Street entrance to Grant Park. On December 3,

1918, the City of Atlanta honored General John J. Pershing, leader of the World War I American Expeditionary Force, by renaming the triangular park at Peachtree and West Peachtree (then Goldsboro Park) to "Pershing Point."[626]

The Ershine Memorial Fountain was the second monument to adorn the intersection of Peachtree and West Peachtree streets, but was moved to Grant Park in 1912.

The Oglethorpe-Hearst Connection:

Oglethorpe University was revived in 1912, after having shut its doors due to the Civil War and then again in 1872 for financial reasons.[627] In 1913, the current site on Peachtree Road was purchased, and the university began classes in 1916.[628] Interestingly enough, one of the larger benefactors of the university was William Randolph Hearst who was given an honorary degree from the school in 1927.[629] Phoebe Hearst Hall is named after his mother.[630] Not to shy away from the random fact, renowned poet Sidney Lanier, after whom Georgia's Lake Lanier was named, graduated from the original Oglethorpe University.[631]

Tales of the Crypt:

On May 26, 1940, a time capsule, the Crypt of Civilization, was sealed at Oglethorpe University.[632] The crypt contains "books on microfilm, recorded music and speeches, a phonograph, a radio, models of hair styles, a pint of beer, a bottle of Coca-Cola, a type-writer and numerous articles of everyday use."[633] Additionally, Garrett reports that "[a] complete description of the crypt, giving its exact location, has been translated into every known language and sent to libraries all over the world."[634] The crypt is set to be opened in 8113.[635]

The Leo Frank Case:

The Leo Frank case was one of the most egregious cases of anti-Semitism in American history. It is a stark reminder of why we should know our history. Garrett's account of the travesty is as follows:

The 13 year-old Mary Phagan was murdered on Saturday, April 25, 1913, at the National Pencil Company building at 39 South Forsyth Street between Alabama and Hunter streets.[636]

Mary Phagan lived with her mother and step-father, Mr. and Mrs. J. W. Coleman, at 146 Lindsay Street near Bankhead Avenue.[637] Phagan's job at the pencil company was to attach the metal eraser tips to the pencils.[638] The metal raw material had run out, so Mary had not been at work for a week.[639] She was due $1.20 however, and Saturday was pay-day. She went to the facility that fateful day to collect it.[640]

She reached the factory at noon and asked Leo Frank, the superintendent, for her pay.[641] Frank was the only one on the office floor of the building; there were two workmen on the fourth floor.⁶⁴² At his trial, Frank testified that he gave her her money and she left.⁶⁴³ Tragically, since Frank was the only one on the office floor, there was no one else who could back up his testimony.

At 3:00 a.m. Sunday morning, the night watchman, Newt Lee discovered Mary Phagan's body in the basement of the building and called the police.⁶⁴⁴ Phagan had been strangled by a cord around her neck and two notes were found next to the body.⁶⁴⁵ One read, verbatim: "Mom that negro fire down here did this when i went to make water and he push me down a hole a long tall black negro did it i right while play with me."⁶⁴⁶ The other note read, verbatim: "He said he would love me, laid down play like the night-witch did it, but that long tall black negro boy did hisself."⁶⁴⁷

Mary Phagan was buried in the Citizen's Cemetery of Marietta.⁶⁴⁸ Frank was indicted for murder May 24, 1913, and entered a plea of not guilty.⁶⁴⁹ About the same time Frank was indicted, James Conley, an African-American man who was a sweeper at the pencil factory was arrested when he was "found washing a shirt, thought to be bloody, on the premises."⁶⁵⁰ Garrett writes that he would be "the principal and most damaging witness against Leo Frank."⁶⁵¹ Conley is described by Garrett as a "dissolute character who had been in and out of the chain gang several times."⁶⁵²

Frank was born in Paris, Texas, on April 17, 1884. The family then moved to Brooklyn when he was three months old.⁶⁵³ Frank graduated from Cornell University in 1906 with a degree in mechanical engineering. In October, 1907, at the request of several Atlanta businessmen, he came to Atlanta to discuss with them the opening of a local pencil factory.⁶⁵⁴ Frank then went to Europe for nine months to study the pencil business.[655] He returned to Atlanta in 1908, and had been the superintendent of the pencil factory since that time.[656]

Chief counsel for Frank was Luther Z. Rosser, Sr. Solicitor General Hugh M. Dorsey, age 42, led the prosecution.[657] Frank A. Hooper, Sr., was assistant counsel to Dorsey.[658]

The trial began July 28, 1913.[659] The presiding judge, Leonard S. Roan, had practiced with Rosser, Leo Frank's attorney, from 1883 through 1887, in the firm of Roan & Rosser.[660]

Both Lee and Conley testified against Frank at the trial. Frank's trial, was widely reported as a complete circus with the courtroom and streets outside filled with an angry mob cheering for the prosecution.

Frank, professing innocence, denounced Conley's testimony as a complete fabrication.[661] In closing, he said to the jury: "Gentlemen, I know nothing whatever of the death of little Mary Phagan. I had no part in causing her death nor do I know how she came to her death after she took her money and left my office. I never even saw Conley in the factory or anywhere else on April 26, 1913."[662]

Frank was found guilty and sentenced to death by hanging.[663] A motion for a new trial was denied and the ruling was affirmed by the Georgia Supreme Court by a divided vote of 4-to-2 on February 17, 1914.[664]

On April 16, 1914, a stay of execution was granted on a motion for a new trial, which was then denied.[665] The case was taken to the U. S. Supreme

Court on a writ of error which was also decided against Frank.[666] At that point, Frank's attorneys appealed to then Governor John M. Slaton for a commutation, which he granted.[667] Slaton received 1,000 letters threatening his life if he commuted the sentence.[668] Particularly significant in Governor Slaton's decision was a letter written to him by Judge Roan a year prior.[669] Roan wrote "I shall ask the prison commission to recommend, and the Governor to commute, Frank's sentence to life imprisonment."[670] He further wrote "[a]fter many months of continued deliberation I am still uncertain of Frank's guilt."[671]

Governor Slaton announced the commutation on June 21, 1914, the night after Frank had been taken to the State Prison in Milledgeville.[672] In response to the commutation, a violent mob gathered in the woods behind Governor Slaton's Buckhead estate that same day, and attacked at the front entrance.[673] Two National Guard companies under the command of Asa Warren Candler fended them off.[674] The mob made another attack that night by setting a fire to a small shack across Peachtree Street as a diversionary tactic.[675] Garrett writes that the mob occupied the woods near the governor's estate for several nights.[676] Candler apprehended 26 of the men and confiscated pistols and dynamite.[677]

A year later, on July 17, 1915, Frank was attacked in prison by a fellow inmate and his throat was slashed.[678] Frank survived this brutal attack.

This aerial photo, taken of Buckhead in 1949, shows the Buckhead estate of Governor John M. Slaton (to the left of Peachtree Road which bisects the photograph). Pharr Road runs parallel to the bottom of the photograph. The section of Pharr Road west of Peachtree was not yet built at the time the photo was taken. Governor Slaton's estate was attacked by a mob which occupied the woods nearby when Governor Slaton commuted the death sentence of Leo Frank. (Photo courtesy of Georgia State University Library).

The most horrendous aspect of the Leo Frank story occurred on Monday, August 16, 1915, when a mob of 25 men in eight cars from the Marietta vicinity traveled to the Georgia state prison at Milledgeville.[679] They arrived at 10:00 p.m., cut the telephone wires, detained the warden, and overpowered the guards on duty.[680] Five men entered the building where Frank was sleeping and carried him out to their cars.[681] The mob lynched Frank that night and left Frank's body hanging from an oak tree about 2.5 miles outside Marietta.[682] Frank was buried at the Mount Carmel Cemetery in Brooklyn.[683] The identity of the 25 men who traveled to Milledgeville and who lynched Leo Frank was not known until January, 2000, when the Phagan-Keen list was published online and listed the names of the men allegedly involved. The Georgia State Board of Pardons and Paroles granted a pardon to Frank posthumously on March 11, 1986.[684]

Fed Up Down South:

The Federal Reserve Banking Act was passed on December 23, 1913, during the first administration of President Woodrow Wilson.[685] The Act divided the country into 12 districts and mandated that the national banks in each district form a district reserve bank with capital of at least $4,000,000.00.[686] State banks and trust companies were permitted to join.[687]

The Federal Commission recommended that all of the Federal Reserve Banks be located *north* of the Ohio and Potomac rivers.[688] A committee was formed at the Atlanta Chamber of Commerce to ask that one of the district reserve banks to be located in Atlanta.[689]

Senator M. Hoke Smith of Georgia and a senator from Texas appealed directly to Woodrow Wilson and "by his intervention [the plan] was changed so as to locate Federal Reserve Banks in Richmond, Atlanta and Dallas."[690] The original location of the Atlanta District Federal Reserve Bank was in the Hurt building.[691]

The Cotton Standard:

The South's economy was largely still based on cotton in 1914.[692] When World War I broke out, this closed overseas markets and also caused a majority of the cotton exchanges in the country to close.[693] "Cotton began to pile up on the streets of Georgia towns."[694] On August 10, 1914, directors of the Atlanta Chamber of Commerce, bankers and other local business leaders formed a committee to address the crisis.[695]

At the committee's first meeting, member J. K. Ottley offered a resolution which in part asked the federal government to allow banks to "offer notes secured by cotton in warehouses as a basis of circulation."[696] The committee submitted a form of warehouse receipt to be used for stored cotton, which receipts could be used as collateral for borrowing money. According to Garrett, the measure was adopted.[697]

Emory University: Mother of Georgia Tech:

The first iteration of Emory University was the Methodist's Georgia Conference Manual Labor School which opened in Covington, Georgia in March, 1835, with 30 students.[698] Early on, the school's president, Dr. Ignatius A. Few, advised the board of trustees that he wanted to greatly expand the school.[699] The Georgia Methodist Conference consented and the state legislature chartered the college on December 10, 1836.[700] The college town of Oxford was developed outside of Covington, Georgia to accommodate the new college.[701] The school was named for Bishop John Emory who was "one of the most scholarly and progressive spirits in southern Methodism, [and] who in 1835 had been thrown from his carriage and killed near his home in Baltimore, Maryland."[702]

Isaac S. Hopkins, the "father of technological education in Georgia" graduated from Emory College in 1859.[703] In 1886, due to his exceptional work in the field of engineering, Hopkins was tapped to organize a state engineering school.[704] That engineering school was organized and became the Georgia Institute of Technology. Accordingly, Emory is often referred to as the "mother of Georgia Tech."[705]

Emory College closed in 1861 due to the Civil War and reopened in 1866. During the war, the school's buildings were used as Confederate hospitals.[706] Today, it is a two-year liberal arts college known as Emory-at-Oxford. It operates under the Emory University aegis.

The Role of Candler in Emory's Becoming a University:

Warren A. Candler, a bishop in the Methodist Church and one of Asa Candler's younger brothers, had attended Emory College with the financial help of his older brother.[707] Warren Candler became the president of Emory College in 1888, and Asa Candler became a member of its board of trustees in 1899.[708]

Emory's road to becoming a university began as a result of a dispute in Tennessee over control of Vanderbilt University. The fight was between the Vanderbilt's Board of Trustees and the Methodist Episcopal Church, South.[709] The courts ruled in favor of the board.[710] At the next General Conference, the Methodists elected the Educational Commission to establish not one, but two "connectional universities," one east and one west of the Mississippi, as a response to the church's loss of Vanderbilt.[711] Southern Methodist University of Dallas, Texas, became the university west of the Mississippi.[712]

Soon after, an Asa Candler company, offered a site in Druid Hills for the east-of-the-Mississippi university. The Atlanta Chamber of Commerce concurrently offered the Methodists $500,000.00 if they would locate it in Atlanta.[713]

At the July 16, 1914 meeting of the Methodist's Education Commission (of which Asa Candler was a member), Asa Candler offered $1,000,000 toward the endowment if the new university was located in Atlanta.[714] The expansion of Emory College became a part of this plan, and the offer was immediately accepted.[715] Prior to this, Candler had written the bishop that the establishment of the church educational institution was "the paramount purpose now of [his] life."[716]

On January 25, 1915, the charter was granted and on June 28, 1915, Asa G. Candler granted 75 acres at Clifton and North Decatur roads for the campus, the acreage being formerly known as Guess Place.[717]

A Dark Period in Atlanta History:

On Thanksgiving Day 1915, William Joseph Simmons, along 33 with other men, climbed to the top of Stone Mountain at midnight and resurrected the Knights of the Ku Klux Klan.[718] Simmons was a preacher, traveling salesman and a promoter of fraternal orders.[719] Two of the men present that night had been members of the original Klan which had been dormant since the 1870's.[720] The State of Georgia actually issued a charter for the organization shortly thereafter.[721] In 1921, the Klan purchased a house at the southwest corner of Peachtree and East Wesley roads in Atlanta and established it as its "Imperial Palace."[722] The site is now the location of Christ the King Church. In 1947, the State of Georgia revoked the Klan charter, but other similar organizations such as the Association of Georgia Klans sprang up in its place.[723]

Egleston Does Right By The Kids:

A native of Charleston, South Carolina, Thomas Egleston came to Atlanta at the age of 14 in 1870 and went to work as a bookkeeper for a mill on Marietta Street.[724] Two years later, he began working for James H. Low & Son in the insurance business.[725] In 1876, the Lows moved to New Orleans and turned their business in Atlanta over to Egleston.[726] In 1883, he became a special agent for the Hartford and moved up the ranks, and in 1909, he persuaded Hartford to move all its operations to Atlanta.[727] When Egleston died a bachelor at the age of 60 in 1916, he left generous sums to his friends and domestic employees.[728] The remainder of his estate, however, was left for the establishment of a children's hospital. Garrett writes that "[i]n his time our hospitals had little or no room for children - when they were sick they usually stayed at home...[and] many children died for the lack of proper attention."[729]

The location originally planned for the children's hospital was a lot on Spring Street, which was purchased in 1919. Due to increasing traffic, the trustees sold this parcel and bought the land where the Emory-area facility is currently located.[730] The land itself had been part of a larger estate that had been bought for back taxes by a "yankee major" while the owner, a Confederate soldier, was fighting in the Civil War.[731] The soldier was able to salvage about 20 acres, and it was this property on which Egleston was originally located.[732] It was named for Henrietta Egleston, Thomas's mother

Made in Atlanta, the Hanson Motor Car:

The Hanson Six automobile made its debut at the Southeastern Automobile Show in Atlanta on February 27, 1917.[733] The car was designed by Don M. Ferguson, an engineer who had worked for both Studebaker and General Motors.[734] The company was located at Murphy Avenue and Sylvan Road (then Ashby Street).[735] The *Atlanta Journal* reported that the company intended to manufacture 2,000 cars its first year and had more than twice that many orders.[736] Hanson promoted the fact that it was 1,000 miles closer to the consumer than other manufacturers in the North and West, and that freight costs were reduced from 75-to-80 percent.[737] Garrett writes that the "Hanson Six was a good automobile" and that it "sold pretty well, especially in Atlanta and the South" but that, by the mid-1920's, competition from the large manufacturers had become too intense and led to the company's demise in 1925.[738]

The Hanson Six represented Atlanta's first foray into the automobile manufacturing arena. This Hanson Six is on display at the Atlanta History Center.

From the Don't Try This at Home Files:

On Wednesday afternoon, July 11, 1917, a group of Woodmen of the World gathered at Piedmont Park with their families for a parade, drills and the flight of a small aircraft taking off and landing at the park.[739] Flight instructor Walker J. Carr took off from the area of the park where a racetrack was then located but was unable to clear a tree on the far side of the track and crashed.[740] According to Garrett, pieces of the plane remained lodged in the tree for months afterward.[741] Fortunately, Carr was practically uninjured, even though he fell some distance to the ground, and was quoted as saying "a little fall like that is all in the day's work and not a thing to worry over."[742]

The Decider: The Man Who Laid Out Peachtree Road:

Meredith Collier was born on May 10, 1782, in Randolph County, North Carolina.[743] He and his wife Elizabeth moved to northeast Georgia in approximately 1806.[744] Their fifth child was George Washington Collier.[745]

In 1823, Meredith Collier was hired, among others, to "designate the different routes on which roads are intended to pass through the county."[746] Peachtree and Shallowford roads were two of the roads Collier was hired to lay out.[747] The original Peachtree Road ran "slightly east of the present Peachtree Road, following an old Indian trail and survived as the long drive to Collier's house until Ansley Park was constructed in 1904 and Sherwood Forest in 1949."[748] Shallowford Road was built to connect Decatur with the Shallow Ford on the Chattahoochee River, which is now submerged under Bull Sluice Lake in Roswell.[749]

In 1823, the county officials had Meredith Collier survey what would become Montgomery Ferry Road that was to run from Decatur to Standing Peachtree on the Chattahoochee River.[750] James McConnell Montgomery opened a ferry at Standing Peachtree, which later was named Defoors Ferry after the ferry's subsequent owner, Martin Defoor.[751] A description of the early Montgomery Ferry Road is as follows:

> **Although it is difficult to trace the entire route of this road today, it left the Shallowford Road (now Clairmont Road) north of Decatur and survives generally in the existing routes of North Decatur Road, Rock Springs Road in Morningside, and continuing along Montgomery Ferry Road through Piedmont Heights into Ansley Park. After crossing Clear Creek in Land Lot 104, the route of the road as it continued in a northwesterly direction has been obliterated by modern development but can be picked up again in Collier Road, which took its name from Meredith's son Andrew Jackson Collier, and DeFoor's Ferry Road, which was named for a subsequent ferry operator at Standing Peachtree.[752]**

George Washington Collier and Ansley Park:

Meredith Collier's son, George, was appointed postmaster of Marthasville (now Atlanta) in 1845. One week later, he bought a small lot at the northwest corner of the intersection of Decatur, Marietta, Peachtree and Whitehall streets, soon to be "Five Points."[753] He then built and began operating a grocery store at this site.[754]

George purchased his brother Edwin's property along Peachtree to the north and another 40 acres in 1884.[755] With these two purchases added to his holdings, Collier owned 700 contiguous acres stretching from just north of

15th Street to Peachtree Creek, where Peachtree Battle Avenue is located today.[756]

Collier had purchased a lot prior to 1868, at the southeast corner of Peachtree and Ellis streets.[757] After Collier's wife died in 1889, Collier constructed a hotel on the site called the Aragon Hotel.[758] Most of the hotels were located around the Union (railroad) Station, which was several blocks to the south, such that some Atlantans thought it was a risky move.[759] The hotel was a success, however, and provided a steady income for Collier's children.[760] The hotel was torn down in 1930.[761]

George Collier died at his home on June 19, 1903.[762] Collier's will had required that the property be kept intact, but the will was set aside by the courts due to contradictory qualifications.[763] On April 24, 1904, the Southern Real Estate Improvement Company purchased Land Lot 105 (202.5 acres), a large part of Collier's estate, for $292,520.[764] Collier had paid $150 for the property.[765] The Southern Real Estate Improvement Company then developed Ansley Park on this property. Ansley Park was originally to be called Peachtree Gardens, but the name was changed prior to development.[766]

Westminster Drive, LaFayette Drive, and the Prado, originally called "the Prater," reportedly typical of Vienna, were the winning submissions to a street naming contest put on by Edwin P. Ansley in 1904 for the new Ansley Park neighborhood.[767]

That Old House:

The old Montgomery Ferry Road mentioned above, along which Meredith Collier built his first home, fell into disuse and Collier built a new house along Peachtree Road in the 1850's.[768] He deeded 200 acres to his son, George, in 1851 which included the old house.[769] Unfortunately, when a line of earthworks and fortifications were constructed for the Civil War defense of Atlanta, the old Collier house was left just yards outside the line, and the house was likely destroyed or heavily damaged during the fighting.[770] George Collier rebuilt the house in approximately 1868 on the exact same site "but certain aspects of the present building's design and materials point conclusively to a construction date in the third rather than the first quarter of the nineteenth century."[771]

The Collier family sold their interest in land lot 104 (several hundred acres which was known as Collier Woods) in 1946 to Haas & Dodd, a partnership that was comprised of Fair Dodd, Herman J. Haas, L. Engle Mock, Judson W. Garner, Charles A. Meriwether, Sr., Edwin R. Haas, Jr. and Elliot L. Haas.[772] In 1948, Haas & Dodd began developing the Sherwood Forest neighborhood on the land.[773] The developers intended to tear down the Collier house.[774] In October, 1949, Atlanta architect R. Kennon Perry bought two lots in the new subdivision, one of which included the old Collier house, and his original intent, as well, was to tear the house down.[775] If not demolished, the developers required that the house be moved to conform to the new setback lines and that the buyer "remodel the residence to conform to all restrictions of the subdivision."[776]

Perry who, incidentally, supervised construction of the Academy of Medicine at 7th and West Peachtree streets, determined that the Collier house was sound and decided to preserve it.[777] Recognizing the history of the house, and with support from the neighborhood, Perry succeeded in getting permission from the developers to leave the house in its original location.[778]

Perry completely remodeled the house, but the general floor plan remained the same. "Collier's old stove chimneys, fireplaces and cellar; the walnut trees in the backyard; and the old smokehouse survived as well."[779]

Perry died in December, 1957 and his wife sold the house in 1958 to a local banker, but his ownership was short-lived.[780] The banker became Sherwood Forest's Hester Prynne when neighbors discovered the unmarried man had female house mates.[781]

In July 1958, the house was sold to James Bentley, Jr., who was widely known for re-energizing Georgia's Republican Party.[782] Bentley was active in state politics, was elected comptroller general in 1962, and made headlines by switching his affiliation to the Republican party in 1968.[783] Bentley died on November 7, 2003, and the house is now owned by Bentley's daughter and husband who reside there.[784] The house is one of the few antebellum structures in Atlanta.

An interesting aside, Haas & Dodd, the developer of Sherwood Forest neighborhood, in which the Collier house is located, was formed in 1891 and is still in business today. It was involved in the development of the Garden Hills neighborhood and the acquisition of the site which became Lenox Square. Haas & Dodd also brokered some of the land on which the interstates run through Atlanta.

The Bentley House, also known as the Wash Collier House, is a private residence located in the Sherwood Forest neighborhood. The house dates back to the Civil War era. Its first owner was Meredith Collier, the Atlanta pioneer who laid out the route of Peachtree Road.

Atlanta Hosts Georgia's Three Governors Controversy:

In the summer of 1946, Eugene Talmadge won the Democratic *primary* election for governor.[785] Ellis Arnall was the sitting governor.[786] The Republicans did not have a nominee and were not planning on entering a candidate to run against Talmadge in the general election.[787] Talmadge was not in good health and, even before the general election, his supporters feared he might die before his inauguration in January, 1947. Talmadge did indeed die in December, 1946, three weeks before taking office.[788]

After much research, the Talmadge supporters found some dubious constitutional evidence that the state legislature could elect the governor if the governor-elect died before taking office. This opened the possibility that Eugene's son, Herman Talmadge, could be a safe back-up as a write-in candidate.[789] According to their research, the General Assembly could choose between the second and third place vote-getters from the general election.[790] Although Eugene Talmadge had been unopposed on the ballot, there had been several write-in candidates and Talmadge supporters made sure one of them was Herman Talmadge (the back-up plan).[791] The initial write-in ballot count gave James Carmichael 669 votes, D. Talmadge Bowers (a tombstone salesman) 637 votes and Herman Talmadge 617 votes. A highly dubious recount uncovered 56 more votes for Herman Talmadge, four votes more than Carmichael.[792]

The problem with the General Assembly's selecting the governor was that a new state Constitution created the office of lieutenant governor. This post would be filled for the first time in the 1946 election.[793] The new Constitution provided that the lieutenant governor would become the governor if the governor died in office, but it was *not clear* about whether he would succeed the governor if the governor died *before taking office*.[794] Melvin Thompson had been elected lieutenant governor in the 1946 elections.[795]

The General Assembly convened in January, 1947. Since Eugene Talmadge, the actual winner of the election, had died, the Legislature selected Herman Talmadge as the next governor, ignoring Thompson's argument that, under the new Constitution, he should be governor.[796] Thompson appealed to the Georgia Supreme Court and set up headquarters as governor in downtown Atlanta.[797]

The outgoing governor, Ellis Arnall, then announced that he would not relinquish the office until it was clear who the next governor was.[798] Herman Talmadge asked Arnall to respect the General Assembly's decision, but Arnall refused to step aside and maintained that the legislature had no right to elect a governor.[799] Talmadge then ordered state troopers to remove Arnall from the

Capitol.[800] All three claimed to be governor of Georgia. Talmadge seized control of the governor's office and had the locks on the doors changed. Arnall set up a governor's office in an information kiosk in the Capitol.[801] Ultimately, Arnall stepped aside and supported Thompson, but for three days however, Georgia had three governors.[802]

And then there were two. The standoff between Thompson and Talmadge lasted another two months. During that time, both were appointing government officials.[803] In March, 1947, the Georgia Supreme Court ruled that Melvin Thompson was the rightful governor at least until a special election could be held.[804] Within hours, Talmadge capitulated and left the governor's office, but not for long. Talmadge campaigned for, and later won, a 1948 special election for Governor.[805] One of M. E. Thompson's major accomplishments as governor was the acquisition of Jekyll Island (for $675,000).[806]

Appendix 1

The following is a firsthand account of the events surrounding the 1933 kidnapping and safe return of banking executive, J. K. Ottley, as well as the apprehension of the lead kidnapper, William Randolph Delinski, written by Ottley's son, an Atlanta advertising executive and former *Atlanta Journal* reporter. The kidnapping was one of the first, if not the first, executive kidnappings in the country. It followed closely the infamous kidnapping of famous aviator Charles A. Lindbergh's son in March, 1932, and made headlines nationwide.

Father was kidnapped early on the morning of July 6, 1933 by William R. Delinski and Pryor Bowen. My wife, Mary, and I were at the Cloister, Sea Island, Georiga and I was informed of this by a telephone call from my nephew, George W. McCarty, Jr. At first, I thought the call was part of a joke, but realized that George wouldn't joke about something like that.

To get back to Atlanta as fast as possible, I telephoned Harold Elliott, vice president of Eastern Air Lines and asked if he could send a charter plane to pick me up. He said he would get one underway immediately. A. P. Kerr landed in a Kingbird on the strip at Sea Island and we took off immediately for the emergency field at McRae, Georgia, in the hope of catching the regular Jacksonville-Atlanta plane there.

Over the Okefenokee swamp, A. P. waggled his wings violently and I ran up to the cockpit. He had gotten the news over the radio that father had been released. At McRae, I transferred to the regular flight and continued to Atlanta on it. Incidentally, Elliott would never bill me for the charter flight.

At home, I got the full story on the kidnapping. William R. Delinski (name not known until later) and Pryor Bowen got in father's car in the morning at the gate of 3415 Peachtree [now site of Lenox Square Mall] to ride to town with him. They immediately forced him, at pistol point, to get in the back of the car and while Bowen drove, Delinski taped father's eyes and mouth and bound his hands.

They drove into the country near Suwanee, Georgia. Delinski left Bowen with father and drove back to Atlanta to leave a ransom note in the mailbox at *Joyeuse* [the name of their residence at 3415 Peachtree], always a hard name for the street car conductor to pronounce. He then left the car in the Spring Street garage downtown where it was identified on July 12.

In the meantime, Bowen had removed the tape from father's mouth and eyes and allowed him to be more comfortable while waiting for Delinski to return with the ransom money.

Father talked to Bowen and by that afternoon persuaded Bowen to release him.

Father and Bowen walked to a farm house and the farmer drove them to Suwanee where he called the Atlanta Police department and my mother.

As soon as Delinski heard on the radio of father's escape, he left town without going back to his boarding house to pick up his clothes and other belongings. Delinski set up the kidnapping by pretending to assist a man who was operating a fruit stand on the sidewalk in front of the home. This was during the depression. Mother and father gave their permission for the orange stand operation to help a man unable to get a job. Delinski frequently got a ride to town with father under the pretense of going in to buy fruit for the stand. Thus father had no hesitation in letting Delinski get in his car on the morning of the kidnapping. Bowen, whom father had not seen, was hiding behind one of the columns at the gate. Delinski had met Bowen when they spent the night together a few days before the kidnapping at the Wesley Memorial Church dormitory. He took Pryor to Piedmont Park the next day and persuaded him to join the kidnapping. Delinski told Bowen that his name was Collins, but nothing else about himself.

Bowen, of course was in custody but he had no idea where Delinski lived and actually didn't know his real name. It was July 14th before Delinski was identified. On the day prior to the kidnapping, he advised his landlady that he would be out of town for several days. Therefore, she didn't concern herself about Delinski's room until several days after the date for his return. Then the landlady went through his belongings and notified the police that her roomer might be the man for whom they were searching.

By a rare coincidence, I sat next to the son of Delinski's landlady at a dinner of the Atlanta Advertising Club. It was to honor Mary and me on the occasion of my retirement from Liller, Neal, Battle & Lindsey ad agency. The man was advertising manager of Southern Bell Telephone and Telegraph Co. As president of the Ad Club, he presided at the dinner and Mary and I were seated on his right and left.

An FBI operative, D. T. Quinn was assigned full-time to the case and took up residence at Joyeuse. Also, city detectives were assigned full time to guard my children at our duplex at 705 Penn Avenue.

The time prior to Delinski's capture proved to be the most trying of all for father. Law enforcement officers throughout the country were picking up every suspect and of course they wanted father to see and identify them. Many times officers would bring out suspects after midnight.

After [the landlady] turned over Delinski's things to the police, it was easy to place him. He was an ex-sailor and stationery salesman. His parents lived in Miami, Florida, and his mother was prominent in civic work there.

A lookout was established at the Delinski residence and Mrs. Delinski was followed one night when she drove to Ft. Lauderdale, Florida, and mailed a letter and package of clothes to her son care of general delivery at San Antonio, Texas.

The letter contained money to help Delinski get to, and live in, Mexico.

Plans were made immediately for me, Atlanta Chief of Detectives T. O. Sturdevant and Captain Ginn to go to San Antonio and pick up Delinski when he came for his letter. There was argument about the best method of preventing advance newspaper publicity. I prevailed and we gave the whole story in advance to the editors of the Atlanta papers and to those in San Antonio on our arrival. In turn, they withheld publication until after the capture. The San Antonio FBI office kept a watch on the post office there while we were en route.

American Airlines could confirm reservations only from Memphis so we jumped in my car to make a record drive via Nashville (hoping to pick up seats there). If the detectives hadn't been with me, my car would have been stopped a hundred times for speeding and running red lights, especially going through Chattanooga. However, local police did not lift an eyebrow.

We did get plane seats out of Nashville and were all glad we didn't have to drive the rest of the way to Memphis.

Both Delinski and Bowen were tried in Fulton County Superior Court and convicted. The former drew a four to twenty-eight year sentence and the latter one year. Bowen was put on probation after serving six weeks by Judge John D. Humphries.

Everyone thought that Bowen was a young man who had been influenced by an older man and that he would straighten out. This did not happen and Bowen was killed in an attempted holdup in Miami shortly after he was released from jail.

Delinski escaped from the Georgia State Prison at Reidsville. He was apprehended robbing a residence in Cincinnati, Ohio and returned to Reidsville.

He got out once more on a habeas corpus issued by the McDuffie County ordinary court. The Georgia legislature at its next session passed a bill forbidding notaries from hearing or issuing such writs.

Later Delinski's lawyer, Randall Evans, wrote me and asked if I or any other members of the family would oppose an application for parole. I replied that I would let him know later and drove to Reidsville to talk to the warden. I asked him what kind of citizen Delinski was making. He told me that he was <u>causing more trouble than any of the other prisoners</u> he had. The warden said Delinski would be a model prisoner if he spent as much time on assignments as he devoted to trying to get out of doing all of the work he was supposed to do. Naturally, I told the lawyer that I would oppose the parole application and it was not submitted.

James Meriwether Ottley is a 41 year-old real estate lawyer, a fourth generation Atlantan, a resident of Vinings, an humble student of Atlanta history and an ardent admirer of Franklin Garrett and his lifetime of contribution to our city.

All photographs (other than the cover photo and the aerial photograph on page 89) were taken by James M. Ottley.

[1]Garrett, Franklin. Atlanta and Environs: A Chronicle of Its People and Events. Volume II. Athens: Univesity of Georgia Press, 1954; p. 24.
[2]Ibid.
[3]Ibid.
[4]Ibid.
[5]Ibid.
[6]Ibid; p.28.
[7]Ibid.
[8]Ibid.
[9]Ibid.
[10]Ibid.
[11]Ibid.
[12]Ibid.
[13]Ibid; p.29.
[14]Ibid;
[15]Ibid.
[16]Sophia B. Packard. (2012). Biography.com. 6/12/2012. <http://www.biography.com>. sophia-b-packard-40659; p.29.Garrett, Franklin. Atlanta and Environs: A Chronicle of Its People and Events. Volume II. Athens: University of Georgia Press, 1954; p.29.
[17]Garrett, Franklin. Atlanta and Environs: A Chronicle of Its People and Events. Volume II. Athens: University of Georgia Press, 1954;
[18]Ibid; p.41.
[19]Atlanta Preservation Center. "LP Grant Mansion." 6/12/2012. <http://www.atlantapresenvationcenter.com/grant_mansion>.
[20]Ibid.
[21]Ibid.
[22]Ibid.
[23]Ibid.
[24]Garrett, Franklin. Atlanta and Environs: A Chronicle of Its People and Events. Volume II. Athens: University of Georgia Press, 1954; p. 882.
[25]Ibid; p. 46.
[26]Ibid.
[27]Ibid; p. 48.
[28]Ibid; p. 47.
[29]Ibid; p. 49.
[30]Ibid; p. 55.
[31]Ibid; p. 58.
[32]Ibid.
[33]Ibid.
[34]Ibid.
[35]Ibid; p. 61.
[36]Wikipedia. "Kimball House (Atlanta)." 8/7/2012. <http://www.wikipedia.org/wiki/kimball_house_(Atlanta,_Georgia); p. 2.

[37] Ibid.
[38] Garrett, Franklin. <u>Atlanta and Environs: A Chronicle of Its People and Events</u>. Volume II. Athens: University of Georgia Press, 1954; p. 61.
[39] Ibid.
[40] Ibid.
[41] <u>Wikipedia</u>. "Kimball House (Atlanta)." 8/7/2012. <http://www.wikipedia.org/wiki/kimball_house_(Atlanta,_Georgia); p. 2.
[42] Ibid.
[43] Garrett, Franklin. <u>Atlanta and Environs: A Chronicle of Its People and Events</u>. Volume II. Athens: University of Georgia Press, 1954; p. 61.
[44] Ibid; p. 62.
[45] Ibid.
[46] Ibid.
[47] Ibid.
[48] Ibid.
[49] Ibid; p. 70.
[50] Ibid; p. 71.
[51] Ibid.
[52] Ibid; p. 77.
[53] Ibid.
[54] Ibid; p. 78.
[55] Ibid.
[56] Ibid.
[57] Ibid.
[58] Ibid; p. 197.
[59] Ibid; p. 198.
[60] <u>Stone Quarries and Beyond</u>. "Structures and Monuments in Which Georgia Stone Was Used." 6/18/2012. <http://www.quarriesandbeyond.org>; p. 5.
[61] Garrett, Franklin. <u>Atlanta and Environs: A Chronicle of Its People and Events</u>. Volume II. Athens: University of Georgia Press, 1954; p. 91.
[62] Ibid.
[63] Ibid.
[64] Ibid; p. 93.
[65] Ibid.
[66] Ibid; p. 99.
[67] Ibid.
[68] Ibid; p. 100.
[69] Ibid.
[70] Ibid.
[71] Ibid.
[72] Ibid.
[73] Ibid.
[74] Ibid.
[75] Ibid.
[76] Ibid.

[77] Ibid.
[78] Ibid; p. 101.
[79] Ibid.; p. 100.
[80] Ibid.
[81] Ibid; p. 102.
[82] Ibid;
[83] Ibid.
[84] Ibid.
[85] Ibid.
[86] Cyclorama. "History." 7/10/2012. <http://www.atlantacyclorama.org/history.php>; p. 4.
[87] Cyclorama. "Quick Facts." 7/10/2012. <http://www.atlantacyclorama.org/history.php>; p. 2.
[88] Garrett, Franklin. Atlanta and Environs: A Chronicle of Its People and Events. Volume II. Athens: University of Georgia Press, 1954; p. 110.
[89] Ibid.
[90] Ibid.
[91] Ibid.
[92] Ibid.
[93] Ibid.
[94] Ibid.
[95] Ibid; p. 111.
[96] Ricken, John. The New Georgia Encyclopedia. "Fort McPherson." 6/18/2012. The University of Georgia Press; <http://www.georgiaencyclopedia.org>; p. 1.
[97] Garrett, Franklin. Atlanta and Environs: A Chronicle of Its People and Events. Volume II. Athens: University of Georgia Press, 1954; p. 111.
[98] Ibid.
[99] Ibid.
[100] Ibid.
[101] Ibid.
[102] Ibid.
[103] Ibid; p. 119.
[104] Allen, Frederick. Secret Formula: How Brilliant Marketing and Relentless Salesmanship Made Coca-Cola the Best-Known Product in the World. Harper Collins. 1994; p. 19.
[105] Ibid; p. 21.
[106] Garrett, Franklin. Atlanta and Environs: A Chronicle of Its People and Events. Volume II. Athens: University of Georgia Press, 1954; p. 120.
[107] Ibid.
[108] Allen, Frederick. Secret Formula: How Brilliant Marketing and Relentless Salesmanship Made Coca-Cola the Best-Known Product in the World. Harper Collins. 1994; p. 24.
[109] Ibid.
[110] Ibid; p. 25.
[111] Ibid.

[112] Allen, Frederick. Secret Formula: How Brilliant Marketing and Relentless Salesmanship Made Coca-Cola the Best-Known Product in the World. Harper Collins. 1994; p. 25.
[113] Ibid; p. 23.
[114] Ibid.
[115] Ibid.
[116] Ibid.
[117] Ibid.
[118] Ibid; p. 24.
[119] Ibid.
[120] Ibid; p. 26.
[121] Garrett, Franklin. Atlanta and Environs: A Chronicle of Its People and Events. Volume II. Athens: University of Georgia Press, 1954; p. 121.
[122] Wikipedia. "Coca Cola: 19th Century Historical Origins." 6/12/2012. <http://www.wikipedia.org/wiki/coca-cola#19thcentury_historical_origins>.
[123] Allen, Frederick. Secret Formula: How Brilliant Marketing and Relentless Salesmanship Made Coca-Cola the Best-Known Product in the World. Harper Collins. 1994; p. 26.
[124] Ibid; p. 27.
[125] Ibid.
[126] Ibid.
[127] Allen, Frederick. Secret Formula: How Brilliant Marketing and Relentless Salesmanship Made Coca-Cola the Best-Known Product in the World. Harper Collins. 1994; p. 27.
[128] Ibid.
[129] Ibid; p. 28.
[130] Garrett, Franklin. Atlanta and Environs: A Chronicle of Its People and Events. Volume II. Athens: University of Georgia Press, 1954; p. 121.
[131] Ibid.
[132] Ibid.
[133] Ibid.
[134] Allen, Frederick. Secret Formula: How Brilliant Marketing and Relentless Salesmanship Made Coca-Cola the Best-Known Product in the World. Harper Collins. 1994; p. 28.
[135] Garrett, Franklin. Atlanta and Environs: A Chronicle of Its People and Events. Volume II. Athens: University of Georgia Press, 1954; p. 122.
[136] Allen, Frederick. Secret Formula: How Brilliant Marketing and Relentless Salesmanship Made Coca-Cola the Best-Known Product in the World. Harper Collins. 1994; p. 30.
[137] Garrett, Franklin. Atlanta and Environs: A Chronicle of Its People and Events. Volume II. Athens: University of Georgia Press, 1954; p. 122.
[138] Ibid.
[139] Ibid.
[140] Ibid.

[141] Allen, Frederick. Secret Formula: How Brilliant Marketing and Relentless Salesmanship Made Coca-Cola the Best-Known Product in the World. Harper Collins. 1994; p. 30.
[142] Wikipedia. "Coca Cola: 19th Century Historical Origins." 6/12/2012. <http://www.wikipedia.org/wiki/coca-cola#19thcentury_historical_origins>.
[143] Ibid.
[144] Garrett, Franklin. Atlanta and Environs: A Chronicle of Its People and Events. Volume II. Athens: University of Georgia Press, 1954; p. 122.
[145] Allen, Frederick. Secret Formula: How Brilliant Marketing and Relentless Salesmanship Made Coca-Cola the Best-Known Product in the World. Harper Collins. 1994; p. 33.
[146] Garrett, Franklin. Atlanta and Environs: A Chronicle of Its People and Events. Volume II. Athens: University of Georgia Press, 1954; p. 122.
[147] Ibid.
[148] Ibid.
[149] Allen, Frederick. Secret Formula: How Brilliant Marketing and Relentless Salesmanship Made Coca-Cola the Best-Known Product in the World. Harper Collins. 1994; p. 34.
[150] Garrett, Franklin. Atlanta and Environs: A Chronicle of Its People and Events. Volume II. Athens: University of Georgia Press, 1954; p. 122.
[151] Allen, Frederick. Secret Formula: How Brilliant Marketing and Relentless Salesmanship Made Coca-Cola the Best-Known Product in the World. Harper Collins. 1994; p. 32.
[152] Ibid; p. 31.
[153] Ibid; p. 32.
[154] Ibid.
[155] Ibid.
[156] Ibid.
[157] Ibid; p. 32.
[158] Ibid; p. 34.
[159] Ibid.
[160] Garrett, Franklin. Atlanta and Environs: A Chronicle of Its People and Events. Volume II. Athens: University of Georgia Press, 1954; p. 123.
[161] Ibid.
[162] Ibid.
[163] Ibid; p. 124.
[164] Ibid.
[165] Ibid.
[166] Ibid.
[167] Ibid.
[168] Ibid; p. 125.
[169] Allen, Frederick. Secret Formula: How Brilliant Marketing and Relentless Salesmanship Made Coca-Cola the Best-Known Product in the World. Harper Collins. 1994; p. 39.
[170] Ibid.

[171]Ibid.
[172]Ibid.
[173]Allen, Frederick. Secret Formula: How Brilliant Marketing and Relentless Salesmanship Made Coca-Cola the Best-Known Product in the World. Harper Collins. 1994; p. 51.
[174]Ibid; p. 52.
[175]Ibid.
[176]Ibid.
[177]Ibid; p. 58.
[178]Garrett, Franklin. Atlanta and Environs: A Chronicle of Its People and Events. Volume II. Athens: University of Georgia Press, 1954; p. 767.
[179]Ibid.
[180]Ibid.
[181]Ibid; p. 768.
[182]Allen, Frederick. Secret Formula: How Brilliant Marketing and Relentless Salesmanship Made Coca-Cola the Best-Known Product in the World. Harper Collins. 1994; p. 41.
[183]Ibid.
[184]Ibid.
[185]Ibid.
[186]Ibid.
[187]Ibid.
[188]Ibid; p. 42.
[189]Ibid.
[190]Ibid.
[191]Ibid; p. 43.
[192]Ibid; p. 45.
[193]Ibid.
[194]Ibid.
[195]Ibid.
[196]Ibid.
[197]Ibid; p. 46.
[198]Ibid.
[199]Ibid.
[200]Ibid.
[201]Ibid; p. 47.
[202]Ibid; pgs. 47-48.
[203]Ibid; p. 48.
[204]Ibid; p. 49.
[205]Garrett, Franklin. Atlanta and Environs: A Chronicle of Its People and Events. Volume II. Athens: University of Georgia Press, 1954; p. 125.
[206]Ibid.
[207]Ibid.
[208]Ibid.

[209] Allen, Frederick. Secret Formula: How Brilliant Marketing and Relentless Salesmanship Made Coca-Cola the Best-Known Product in the World. Harper Collins. 1994; p. 106.
[210] Ibid.
[211] Ibid.
[212] Ibid.
[213] Ibid.
[214] Ibid.
[215] Ibid; p. 107.
[216] Ibid.
[217] Ibid; p. 108.
[218] Ibid; p. 109.
[219] Garrett, Franklin. Atlanta and Environs: A Chronicle of Its People and Events. Volume II. Athens: University of Georgia Press, 1954; p. 126.
[220] Ibid.
[221] Ibid.
[222] Ibid.
[223] Allen, Frederick. Secret Formula: How Brilliant Marketing and Relentless Salesmanship Made Coca-Cola the Best-Known Product in the World. Harper Collins. 1994; p. 108.
[224] Ibid; p. 112.
[225] Ibid.
[226] Ibid.
[227] Ibid.
[228] Ibid.
[229] Ibid.
[230] Ibid.
[231] Ibid.
[232] Ibid.
[233] Ibid.
[234] Ibid.
[235] Ibid.
[236] Ibid.
[237] Ibid.
[238] Ibid; p. 113.
[239] Garrett, Franklin. Atlanta and Environs: A Chronicle of Its People and Events. Volume II. Athens: University of Georgia Press, 1954; p. 136.
[240] Ibid.
[241] Ibid; p. 137.
[242] Ibid.
[243] Ibid; p. 138.
[244] Ibid.
[245] Ibid.
[246] Ibid; p. 155.
[247] Ibid; p. 141.

[248] Ibid.
[249] Ibid; p. 143.
[250] The New Georgia Encyclopedia. "1887 Piedmont Exposition Main Building." 4/12/2012. The University of Georgia Press. <http://www.georgiaencyclopedia.org>; p. 1.
[251] Jones, Tommy H. Tomitronics. "G.W. Collier House (c. 1868)." 2/27/2012. <http://www.tomitronics.com>; p. 7.
[252] Wikipedia. "Piedmont Exposition: Founding of the Piedmont Exposition Company." 4/12/2012. <http://www.wikipedia.org>; p. 1. (Citing "National Register Information System." National Register of Historic Places. National Park Service, 2007-01-23. http://www.nrhp.focus.nps.gov./natreg/docs/all-data.html>).
[253] Jones, Tommy H. Tomitronics. "G.W. Collier House (c. 1868)." 2/27/2012. <http://www.tomitronics.com>; p. 7.
[254] Garrett, Franklin. Atlanta and Environs: A Chronicle of Its People and Events. Volume II. Athens: University of Georgia Press, 1954; p. 155.
[255] Ibid.
[256] Ibid.
[257] Ibid.
[258] Ibid; p. 157.
[259] Ibid.
[260] Ibid; p. 454.
[261] Ibid.
[262] Ibid.
[263] Ibid; p. 455.
[264] Ibid.
[265] Ibid; p. 158.
[266] Ibid.
[267] Ibid.
[268] Ibid; p. 169.
[269] Ibid.
[270] Ibid; p. 169.
[271] Ibid.
[272] Ibid.
[273] Ibid.
[274] Ibid.
[275] Ibid.
[276] Ibid.
[277] Ibid; p. 170.
[278] Ibid.
[279] Ibid.
[280] Ibid.
[281] Ibid; p. 172.
[282] Ibid; p. 174.
[283] Wikipedia. "Bobby Dodd Stadium." 2/21/2012. <http://www.wikipedia.org>; pgs. 1-2. (Citing "Boddy Dodd Stadium at Historic Grant Field: A Cornerstone of College

Football for Nearly a Century." *RamblinWreck.com*. Georgia Tech Athletic Association. <http://ramblinwreck.cstv.com/genrel/071001aaa.html>. Retrieved March 24, 2007.
[284] Ibid.
[285] Ibid.
[286] Garrett, Franklin. <u>Atlanta and Environs: A Chronicle of Its People and Events</u>. Volume II. Athens: University of Georgia Press, 1954; p. 184.
[287] Ibid.
[288] Ibid; p. 186.
[289] Ibid.
[290] Ibid.
[291] Ibid; p. 194.
[292] Ibid.
[293] Ibid.
[294] Ibid.
[295] Ibid.
[296] Ibid; p. 185.
[297] Ibid; p. 195.
[298] Ibid.
[299] Ibid.
[300] Ibid.
[301] Ibid; p. 185.
[302] Ibid.
[303] Ibid; p. 195.
[304] Ibid.
[305] Ibid; p. 175.
[306] Ibid; p. 209.
[307] Ibid.
[308] Ibid; p. 210.
[309] Ibid.
[310] Ibid.
[311] Ibid.
[312] Ibid.
[313] Ibid.
[314] Ibid.
[315] Ibid; p. 225.
[316] Ibid; p. 210.
[317] Ibid.
[318] Ibid.
[319] Ibid; p. 211.
[320] Ibid; p. 223.
[321] Ibid; p. 222.
[322] Ibid.
[323] Ibid.

[324] Historic College Park Neighborhood Association. "About College Park, Georgia." 6/11/2012. <http://www.hcpna.org>; p. 1.
[325] Ibid.
[326] Ibid.
[327] Ibid.
[328] Grem, Darren. The New Georgia Encyclopedia. "Henry Grady (1850-1889)." 4/12/2012. The University of Georgia Press. <http://www.georgiaencyclopedia.org>; p. 1.
[329] Garrett, Franklin. Atlanta and Environs: A Chronicle of Its People and Events. Volume II. Athens: University of Georgia Press, 1954; p. 233.
[330] Ibid.
[331] Ibid; p. 258.
[332] Ibid.
[333] Ibid; p. 242.
[334] Jones, Tommy H. Tomitronics. "Atlanta Chapter, D.A.R." Craigie House (1914). <http://www.tomitronics.com/oldbuildings/DARhouse/index.html>; p. 1.
[335] Garrett, Franklin. Atlanta and Environs: A Chronicle of Its People and Events. Volume II. Athens: University of Georgia Press, 1954; p. 242.
[336] Wikipedia. "Longfellow House - Washington's Headquarters National Historic Site." 6/19/2012. <http://www.wikipedia.org>; p. 3. (Citing Levine, Miriam. A Guide to Writers' Homes in New England. Cambridge, Massachusetts: Apple-Wood Press, 1984: pgs. 124-125).
[337] Ibid.
[338] Ibid; p. 4. (Citing Wilson, Susan. Literary Trail of Greater Boston. Boston: Houghton Mifflin Company, 2000: p. 109.
[339] Jones, Tommy H. Tomitronics. "Atlanta Chapter, D.A.R." Craigie House (1914). <http://www.tomitronics.com/oldbuildings/DARhouse/index.html>; p. 1.
[340] Ibid; p. 8.
[341] Ibid.
[342] Ibid.
[343] Ibid.
[344] Ibid; pgs. 8-9.
[345] Ibid; p. 9.
[346] Ibid.
[347] Ibid.
[348] Ibid.
[349] Ibid.
[350] Ibid; p. 10. (Citing "Historic Craigie House," Georgia Magazine, Vol. IX, #5, February-March 1966, p. 21).
[351] Ibid; p. 16.
[352] Ibid.
[353] Ibid.
[354] Ibid; p. 17.
[355] Ibid; p. 18.
[356] Ibid; p. 19.

[357] Garrett, Franklin. Atlanta and Environs: A Chronicle of Its People and Events. Volume II. Athens: University of Georgia Press, 1954; p. 299.
[358] Ibid.
[359] Ibid.
[360] Ibid.
[361] Ibid; p. 313.
[362] Ibid.
[363] Ibid; p. 318.
[364] Ibid; p. 319.
[365] Ibid.
[366] Ibid.
[367] Ibid.
[368] Ibid.
[369] Ibid; p. 330.
[370] Ibid; p. 350.
[371] Ibid.
[372] Ibid.
[373] Ibid.
[374] Ibid.
[375] Ibid.
[376] Ibid; p. 394.
[377] Allen, Frederick. Secret Formula: How Brilliant Marketing and Relentless Salesmanship Made Coca-Cola the Best-Known Product in the World. Harper Collins. 1994; p. 140.
[378] Historic College Park Neighborhood Association. "About College Park, Georgia." 6/11/2012. <http://www.hcpna.org>; p. 2.
[379] Garrett, Franklin. Atlanta and Environs: A Chronicle of Its People and Events. Volume II. Athens: University of Georgia Press, 1954; p. 412.
[380] Ibid.
[381] Ibid.
[382] Ibid; p. 413.
[383] Ibid.
[384] Ibid.
[385] Ibid.
[386] Ibid.
[387] Ibid; p. 28.
[388] Ibid.
[389] Ibid.
[390] Ibid.
[391] Ibid.
[392] Ibid.
[393] Ibid; p. 673.
[394] Ibid.
[395] Ibid; p. 131.
[396] Ibid; p. 749.

[397]Ibid; p. 757.
[398]Ibid.
[399]Ibid; p. 761.
[400]Ibid.
[401]Ibid; p. 771.
[402]Ibid; p. 770.
[403]Ibid; p. 771.
[404]Ibid; p. 606.
[405]Ibid; p. 682.
[406]Ibid; p. 782.
[407]Ibid.
[408]Ibid; p. 783.
[409]Ibid; p. 782.
[410]Ibid; p. 783.
[411]"Citizens Trust Bank: History." 6/12/2012. <http://www.ctbconnect.com/history>; p. 1.
[412]Ibid.
[413]Ibid.
[414]Garrett, Franklin. Atlanta and Environs: A Chronicle of Its People and Events. Volume II. Athens: University of Georgia Press, 1954; p. 191.
[415]Ibid.
[416]Ibid.
[417]Ibid.
[418]Ibid.
[419]Ibid; p. 526.
[420]Ibid.
[421]Ibid; p. 632.
[422]Ibid.
[423]Wikipedia. "Ormewood Park History." 6/27/2012. <http://www.wikipedia.org/wiki/ormewoodpark>; p. 1.
[424]Ibid.
[425]Garrett, Franklin. Atlanta and Environs: A Chronicle of Its People and Events. Volume II. Athens: University of Georgia Press, 1954; p. 788.
[426]Ibid; p. 797.
[427]Ibid; p. 787.
[428]Ibid; p. 803.
[429]Ibid; p. 811.
[430]Ibid; p. 828.
[431]Ibid.
[432]Ibid.
[433]Ibid, p. 457.
[434]Ibid; p. 366.
[435]Ibid; p. 367.
[436]Ibid.
[437]Ibid; p. 540.

[438] Ibid; p. 801.
[439] Ibid.
[440] Ibid.
[441] Ibid; p. 803.
[442] Ibid.
[443] Ibid.
[444] Ibid.
[445] Ibid.
[446] Ibid.
[447] Ibid.
[448] Ibid.
[449] Ibid.
[450] Ibid; p. 804.
[451] Ibid.
[452] Ibid; p. 806.
[453] Ibid.
[454] Ibid; p. 805.
[455] Ibid; p. 806.
[456] Ibid.
[457] Ibid.
[458] Ibid.
[459] Ibid.
[460] Ibid.
[461] Ibid.
[462] Ibid.
[463] Ibid; p. 814.
[464] Ibid; p. 814. (Citing Stead, *Georgia: Unfinished State*, 159).
[465] Ibid.
[466] Ibid.
[467] Ibid.
[468] Ibid; p. 815.
[469] Ibid; p. 820.
[470] Ibid.
[471] Ibid.
[472] Ibid.
[473] Ibid; p. 823.
[474] Ibid; p. 824.
[475] Ibid.
[476] Ibid.
[477] Wikipedia. "Swan House (Atlanta, Georgia)." 6/27/2012. http://www.wikipedia.org/wiki/swan_house_(Atlanta, Georgia)>; p. 1. (Citing "National Register Information System." National Register of Historic Places. National Park Service. 2008-04-15. <http://www.nps>.).
[478] Garrett, Franklin. Atlanta and Environs: A Chronicle of Its People and Events. Volume II. Athens: University of Georgia Press, 1954; p. 833.

[479] Ibid.
[480] Ibid.
[481] Ibid; p. 552.
[482] Ibid.
[483] Ibid; p. 848.
[484] Ibid; p. 851
[485] Ibid; p. 852.
[486] Ibid; p. 854.
[487] Ibid.
[488] Ibid; p. 854.
[489] Ibid.
[490] Ibid; p. 855.
[491] Ibid; p. 856.
[492] Ibid.
[493] Ibid.
[494] Ibid; p. 893.
[495] Ibid.
[496] Ibid; p. 911.
[497] Ibid.
[498] Ibid.
[499] Ibid.
[500] Ibid; p. 912.
[501] Ibid.
[502] Ibid.
[503] Ibid.
[504] Ibid.
[505] Ibid.
[506] Ibid.
[507] Ibid.
[508] Ibid.
[509] Ibid; p. 940.
[510] Ibid.
[511] Ibid.
[512] Ibid; p. 941.
[513] Ibid; p. 940.
[514] Ibid; p. 941.
[515] Ibid.
[516] Ibid.
[517] Ibid.
[518] Ibid.
[519] Ibid; p. 942.
[520] Ibid.
[521] Ibid.
[522] Wikipedia. "Gone With The Wind"
<http//www.en.wikipedia.org/wiki/Gone_with_the_Wind> 10/12/12.

[523] Garrett, Franklin. Atlanta and Environs: A Chronicle of Its People and Events. Volume II. Athens: University of Georgia Press, 1954; p. 950.
[524] Ibid.
[525] Ibid; p. 784.
[526] Ibid.
[527] Ibid; p. 833.
[528] Ibid; p. 977.
[529] Ibid.
[530] Ibid; p. 978.
[531] Wikipedia. "Ernest Dawson." 2/27/2012. http://www.wikipedia.org/wiki/ernest dawson>; p. 2.
[532] Ibid.
[533] Ibid.
[534] Ibid.
[535] Ibid.
[536] Ibid.
[537] Ibid.
[538] Garrett, Franklin. Atlanta and Environs: A Chronicle of Its People and Events. Volume II. Athens: University of Georgia Press, 1954; p. 982.
[539] Ibid.
[540] Ibid; p. 977.
[541] Ibid.
[542] Ibid.
[543] Ibid.
[544] Ibid.
[545] Ibid.
[546] Ibid.
[547] Ibid; p. 422.
[548] Ibid.
[549] Ibid.
[550] Ibid; p. 423.
[551] Ibid.
[552] Ibid; p. 460.
[553] Ibid.
[554] Ibid.
[555] Ibid.
[556] Ibid.
[557] Mitchell, Wright. *Buckhead Reporter*. "Hermi's Bridge: A Love Story." 8/7/2012. <http://www.reporternewspapers.net/2010/02/25/hermi%e2%80%99s-bridge-a-love-story>; p. 1.
[558] Ibid.
[559] Ibid.
[560] Ibid.
[561] Ibid.
[562] Ibid.

[563] Ibid.
[564] Ibid.
[565] Ibid.
[566] Garrett, Franklin. <u>Atlanta and Environs: A Chronicle of Its People and Events</u>. Volume II. Athens: University of Georgia Press, 1954; p. 480.
[567] Ibid.
[568] Ibid; p. 480.
[569] Ibid.
[570] Ibid; p. 481.
[571] Ibid; p. 482.
[572] Ibid.
[573] Ibid.
[574] Ibid.
[575] Ibid.
[576] Ibid; p. 483.
[577] <u>Medical Services Buckhead, Atlanta, Georgia</u>. "Hospitals: Historical Note." 7/10/2012. <http://www.buckhead.net/medical>; p. 2.
[578] Garrett, Franklin. <u>Atlanta and Environs: A Chronicle of Its People and Events</u>. Volume II. Athens: University of Georgia Press, 1954; p. 483.
[579] Ibid; p. 494.
[580] Ibid; p. 498.
[581] Ibid; p. 494.
[582] Ibid; p. 495.
[583] Ibid.
[584] Ibid; p. 496.
[585] Ibid; p. 497.
[586] Ibid.
[587] Ibid.
[588] Ibid; p. 136.
[589] Ibid.
[590] Ibid.
[591] Ibid; p. 498.
[592] Ibid.
[593] Ibid.
[594] Ibid; p. 509.
[595] Ibid; p. 510.
[596] Ibid; p. 525.
[597] Ibid.
[598] <u>Wikipedia</u>. "List of Former Atlanta Street Names." 6/27/2012. <http://www.en.wikipedia.org/hist_of_formerstreet_names>. (Citing Sanborn Fire Map of Atlanta, 1886).
[599] Garrett, Franklin. <u>Atlanta and Environs: A Chronicle of Its People and Events</u>. Volume II. Athens: University of Georgia Press, 1954; p. 509.
[600] Ibid.

[601] Garrett, Franklin. Atlanta and Environs: A Chronicle of Its People and Events. Volume II. Athens: University of Georgia Press, 1954; p. 545.
[602] Ibid.
[603] Ibid; p. 549.
[604] Ibid.
[605] Ibid.
[606] Ibid.
[607] Ibid; p. 563.
[608] Ibid.
[609] Ibid.
[610] Ibid; p. 590.
[611] Ibid.
[612] Ibid.
[613] Ibid; p. 564.
[614] Ibid.
[615] Ibid.
[616] Ibid; p. 342.
[617] Ibid.
[618] Ibid; p. 848.
[619] Ibid; p. 533.
[620] Ibid.
[621] Ibid.
[622] Ibid.
[623] Ibid; p. 591.
[624] Ibid.
[625] Ibid.
[626] Ibid; p. 748.
[627] Ibid; p. 595.
[628] Ibid; p. 596.
[629] Ibid.
[630] Ibid.
[631] Ibid; p. 505.
[632] Ibid; p. 596.
[633] Ibid; p. 597.
[634] Ibid.
[635] Ibid.
[636] Ibid; p. 619.
[637] Ibid.
[638] Ibid.
[639] Ibid.
[640] Ibid.
[641] Ibid.
[642] Ibid.
[643] Ibid.
[644] Ibid.

[645] Ibid.
[646] Ibid.
[647] Ibid.
[648] Ibid.
[649] Ibid.
[650] Ibid.
[651] Ibid.
[652] Ibid; p. 621.
[653] Ibid.
[654] Ibid.
[655] Ibid.
[656] Ibid.
[657] Ibid.
[658] Ibid.
[659] Ibid.
[660] Ibid.
[661] Ibid.
[662] Ibid.
[663] Ibid; p. 624.
[664] Ibid; p. 625.
[665] Ibid; p. 626.
[666] Ibid.
[667] Ibid.
[668] Ibid.
[669] Ibid.
[670] Ibid.
[671] Ibid.
[672] Ibid.
[673] Ibid; p. 627.
[674] Ibid.
[675] Ibid.
[676] Ibid.
[677] Ibid.
[678] Ibid.
[679] Ibid.
[680] Ibid.
[681] Ibid; pgs. 627-628.
[682] Ibid; p. 628.
[683] Ibid.
[684] <http//www.jewishvirtuallibrary.org/jsource/anti-semitism/frank.html.> 10/12/12.
[685] Ibid; p. 635.
[686] Ibid.
[687] Ibid.
[688] Ibid.
[689] Ibid; p. 636.

[690] Ibid.
[691] Ibid; p. 637.
[692] Ibid.
[693] Ibid; p. 636.
[694] Ibid; p. 638.
[695] Ibid.
[696] Ibid.
[697] Ibid.
[698] Ibid; p. 641.
[699] Ibid.
[700] Ibid.
[701] Ibid.
[702] Ibid.
[703] Ibid; p. 642.
[704] Ibid.
[705] Ibid.
[706] Ibid.
[707] Ibid.
[708] Ibid.
[709] Ibid.
[710] Ibid.
[711] Ibid; p. 643.
[712] Ibid.
[713] Ibid.
[714] Ibid; p. 644.
[715] Ibid.
[716] Ibid; p. 643.
[717] Ibid; p. 644.
[718] Ibid; p. 669.
[719] Ibid.
[720] Ibid.
[721] Ibid.
[722] Ibid.
[723] Ibid; p. 670.
[724] Ibid; p. 693.
[725] Ibid.
[726] Ibid.
[727] Ibid; p. 694.
[728] Ibid.
[729] Ibid.
[730] Ibid.
[731] Ibid.
[732] Ibid.
[733] Ibid; p. 706.
[734] Ibid; p. 707.

[735]Ibid.
[736]Ibid.
[737]Ibid.
[738]Ibid.
[739]Ibid; p. 708.
[740]Ibid.
[741]Ibid.
[742]Ibid.
[743]Jones, Tommy H. Tomitronics. "G.W. Collier House (c. 1868)." 2/27/2012. <http://www.tomitronics.com>; p. 1.
[744]Ibid.
[745]Ibid.
[746]Ibid; p. 2.
[747]Ibid.
[748]Ibid; pgs. 2-3.
[749]Ibid; p. 2.
[750]Ibid.
[751]Ibid.
[752]Ibid.
[753]Ibid, p. 3.
[754]Ibid.
[755]Ibid; p. 7.
[756]Ibid.
[757]Ibid; p. 8.
[758]Ibid.
[759]Ibid.
[760]Ibid.
[761]Ibid.
[762]Ibid.
[763]Ibid.
[764]Ibid.
[765]Ibid.
[766]Garrett, Franklin. Atlanta and Environs: A Chronicle of Its People and Events. Volume II. Athens: University of Georgia Press, 1954; p. 457.
[767]Ibid.
[768]Jones, Tommy H. Tomitronics. "G.W. Collier House (c. 1868)." 2/27/2012. <http://www.tomitronics.com>; p. 4.
[769]Ibid.
[770]Ibid; p. 5.
[771]Ibid; p. 6.
[772]Ibid; p. 11.
[773]Ibid.
[774]Ibid; p. 12.
[775]Ibid.
[776]Ibid.

[777]Ibid.

[778]Ibid; p. 13.

[779]Ibid.

[780]Ibid.

[781]Ibid.

[782]Ibid.

[783]Ibid; p. 14.

[784]Ibid.

[785]Buchanan, Scott E. The New Georgia Encyclopedia. "Three Governors Controversy." 5/11/2010. The University of Georgia Press. <http://www.georgiaencycloeida.org/nge/article.jsp?id=h-591>; p. 1.

[786]Ibid.

[787]Ibid.

[788]Ibid.

[789]Ibid.

[790]Ibid.

[791]Ibid.

[792]Our Georgia History. "Georgia's Three Governor's Controversy." 9/11/2012. Golden Ink. <http://www.ourgeorgiahistory.com/ogh/Georgia's_Three_Governor's_Controversey>.; p. 2.

[793]Ibid; p. 1.

[794]Ibid.

[795]Ibid; p. 2.

[796]Ibid.

[797]Ibid.

[798]Ibid.

[799]Ibid.

[800]Ibid.

[801]Ibid.

[802]Ibid.

[803]Ibid.

[804]Ibid.

[805]Georgia Info. "M.E. Thompson State Historical Marker." Digital Library of Georgia. 9/11/2012. <http://www.georgiainfo.qulileo.usg.edu/gahistmarkers/METhompson histmarker.htm>.

[806]Ibid.

Made in the USA
Lexington, KY
28 July 2016